AN INTRODUCTION TO THEORY OF KNOWLEDGE

by
Dr. Russell A. Peterson

All rights reserved. No part of this publication may be reproduced, distributed, or transmitted in any form or by any means, including photocopying, recording, or other electronic or mechanical methods, without the prior written permission of the publisher, except in the case of brief quotations embodied in critical reviews and certain other noncommercial uses permitted by copyright law.

Printed in the United States of America

ISBN 978-1-941489-99-4

www.AudioEnlightenmentPress.com

TABLE of CONTENTS

DEDICATION	i
BOOKS and TRANSLATIONS by Russell A. Peterson	iii
INTRODUCTION	v
CHAPTER ONE The Meaning of Philosophy	1
CHAPTER TWO The Meaning of Science	13
CHAPTER THREE The Meaning of Knowledge	21
CHAPTER FOUR Five Definitions	41
CHAPTER FIVE The Epistemological Stance of Giveness	53
CHAPTER SIX The Reality of the Concept	85
CHAPTER SEVEN The Intellect as Process	115
CHAPTER EIGHT Perception as Knowledge	163
SELECT BIBLIOGRAPHY	203
RESOURCES	211

FOR MY
GRADUATE STUDENTS
WITH DEEPEST RESPECT

BOOKS and TRANSLATIONS

by

Russell A. Peterson

Translations

The God That Job Had

The Synoptic New Testament

Reading the Psalms

Children's Tales From Norway

Books

The Size of Death

Education is a Philosophy

Campus Invocation

Existentialism and the Creative Teacher

Counseling Tips for the Beginning Teacher

Luther For Today

How Love Will Help

Lutheranism and the Educational Ethic

God and I

An Introduction To Theory of Knowledge

The Will in Human Learning

A Dictionary of Philosophical Concepts

INTRODUCTION

There have been very few major works written in the field of epistemology during the past couple of decades. For the learning theorist, this has been unfortunate. The absence is quite evident as we review the writing of these theorists. How thin is learning theory when it has not been grounded on theory of knowledge.

It has not been my intention, however, to write a major work in epistemology, offering something new in theory; moreover, I have not made any attempt to provide an historical perspective of what epistemologists over the past twenty-five years have given us. While questions pertaining to learning theory are to be found on every page of the book, there has not been a studied attempt to 'unite' epistemology and learning theory.

Rather, I have set for my goal a discussion of eight major epistemological problems. I do not pretend to say that all questions raised have been answered for every reader. They have been answered to my satisfaction, however. Perhaps the essence of the discussion will assist you to formulate your own answers.

The first question I raise is this one. I believe that the existence of knowledge is the ability of the mind to interiorize its essence or materials. In what ways, then, can we raise questions about knowledge unless we understand the implicative values inherent in the fact of knowledge? Does this force us to begin with knowledge as a given? To do so would insist we think of the intellective process as the embodiment of a knowledge in order to experience knowledge. Our question then, is knowledge a given?

Two, the product of thought, is this the only means at our disposal for identifying knowledge?

Three, why do we believe that the mind is not a receptor of knowledge?

Four, why do we insist that it is the will that supplies the mind with its power to think?

Five, what is the science of perception? Why is its task to formulate the criteria of reality?

Six, why is it that in perception alone we are able to see why the mind uses meaning to find meaning?

Seven, why does the mind find it necessary to order and provide the cognitive energy for the operant principles which direct the knowing power found in certitude?

Eight, what is really being implied when we say that, to know, means the subject has actualized its object and experienced its meaning?

If there is a theory which may be, in one sense, labelled *new*, in this work on epistemology, it would be in reference to my use of the concept experience. Is there knowledge or meaning unless the mind experiences? is the one question which I hope will be answered for every reader.

Russell A. Peterson

An Introduction to Theory of Knowledge

CHAPTER ONE
THE MEANING OF PHILOSOPHY

The concern of philosophy is with concepts, not with things; things become a concern of philosophy only after their essence has been conceptualized. It is through this process of conceptualization that philosophy becomes, in the words of Whitehead, the critic of fundamental ideas.

To conceptualize is to bring forth ideas inherent in premises. Philosophy is the examination of premises, the quest for that knowledge of reality which explains existence and essence but transcends both by discovering their referential meaning.

With its interest in premises, there is no existent without interest to philosophy; no limit can be placed on its responsibilities. Philosophy strives to assist the learner to experience meaning, in spite of the restrictions of experience Hume wishes to place upon its role. Because of its interest in premises, philosophy is developmental in nature; this is a basic contention of Hegel. It is developmental in nature because it formulates definitions as well as develops their meaningfulness. This process permits the mind to penetrate behind appearance in order to determine the nature of reality. At each step definitions are called for, tested, validated or changed.

In the quest for the knowledge of reality, there is the recognition that in premises lie the potentialities of value. There is another way of saying this and Dewey gives us the clue. He says that the office of philosophy is to project by dialectic, resting supposedly upon self-evident premises, a realm in which the object of completest cognitive certitude is also one with the object of the heart's best aspiration.

This is quite different from the position held by Husserl. He is quite adamant when he says that philosophy must make an absolute beginning. Farber interprets this as meaning that philosophy must make no use initially of the materials of the sciences, or of any of the assumptions of the natural

Chapter One: The Meaning of Philosophy

view of the world. It must attempt to begin without presuppositions.

This would be a good epistemological trick if it could be done, even with methods we might call deductive, descriptive or reflective.

The thinking of Aquinas is closer to our position. Philosophy, says Thomas, begins and ends with facts. Facts are the premises of philosophy. This is a strong protective measure for him. What is more logical than to premise philosophical thought on proven fact? Actually, this means for Aquinas that the most cogent philosophical question is, what is reality? This question must be answered before a fact can be actualized. To experience reality is to validate the philosophical basis of the working hypothesis. What greater role could philosophy have than this? he asks.

In an analysis of Thomistic thought on the meaning of philosophy, we find him raising a number of suppositions. These suppositions encourage us to raise a question or two about the relationship between philosophy and science.

Philosophy rests upon proven facts; it also rests upon the values inherent in those facts. When philosophy seeks to know, it is searching for the fact as value. And, so is science.

Philosophy seeks to discover what is real. To know what is real, the mind must know the meaning of reality. Science must ask and answer the same questions.

Truth for philosophy is to know the meaning of existence and essence. To know meaning is to know the nature of an existent. This is the thrust of the scientific method.

Meaning suggests valuation. Both philosophy and science must concern themselves with the implicative values inherent in meaning. Perhaps what we are implying here is that science, to be scientific, must be philosophically based, and philosophy, to be logically structured, must be scientifically based. Philosophy enables science to ask the right questions; science enables philosophy to know what questions to ask.

Philosophy is the analytical factor which provides the spiritual energy for the intellectual process; it is the essence of consciousness. The methodology found in philosophical analysis aids the mind to determine the relationship between cause and its effects. This is a rational analysis which moves on the experienced qualities of intuitive inferences. In this sense, philosophy makes a commitment to knowledge by means of the power of analytical processes, namely, to function on an empirical plane. This is the only way in which philosophy can deal with reality. Philosophy starts working on the presuppositions of an existent. There is something very real about a presupposition. Essentially, it becomes a dialogue between the thought processes of the mind and the revelatory powers of an object. Such a dialogue demands of philosophy the need to experience meaning; an object and its essence remains meaningless until its material is experienced.

We pause for a moment to permit Weigel and Madden to summarize what has been said thus far about the meaning of philosophy. Philosophy is the thought discipline, they tell us, which proceeds from the real considered in terms of meanings, achieved spontaneously by the mind in its search of the real, to the rational erection of a hierarchical system of principles derived from the meanings achieved, in order, they say, to give the ultimate understanding of reality in as far as it is assimilable by the natural human mind.

For reality to be real, it must hold meaning for the mind. To determine meaning in reality is the responsibility of the mind philosophically based on empirical premises.

Philosophy is a matter of reflection; it is the reflective mind and its thought processes which establishes the working relationship between subject and object, form and function, inference and consequence. It is the reflective thought processes which concentrate on universals and their implicative values. Universal truth serves as the testing ground of reflective thought. For philosophy, universal truth (the embodiment of first principles) is cause. The first step in reflective thought is the search for first principles. Only from cause can certain knowledge evolve.

The goal of science is to assist the mind to know by offering supporting evidence, so what is known cannot be questioned as to its validity. Philosophy goes beyond this; its concern is with what is known and why, as well as with what is known, the result of the learning process. Is to know the same as having learned? is the question raised by philosophy.

To ask such a question is to imply that the mind must always be aware of

Chapter One: The Meaning of Philosophy

its own reflective methodologies, and the distinction must be made between learning as a process and knowledge as a possession.

Descartes tells us that philosophy has as its responsibility the unification of human knowledge. Here is the search for the universal, the identification of cause, and the integration of particulars, all of which depend upon the insightful methodologies structured by the mind and used to determine the essence of the knowable. Philosophy, then, as the mind of reflective thought, provides the starting point which the mind itself must experience cognitively in order to know effects. The epistemological concern of philosophy is with the propositions inherent in effects. Wittgenstein does not hesitate to say that the object of philosophy is to make propositions clear; only in this way can thoughts be clarified. The whole thrust of reflective thought is to think upon itself in order to clarify its own processes.

Man as Learner

The mystery of existence is the mystery of man. To ask the question, why is there a world? is to ask, what is man?

The subject matter of education is man. It is man who learns and uses the material of knowledge for his own growth and development.

Man as learner is man as mind. As mind, he is a rational being, capable of thought. We do not raise the question in the same way Kierkegaard does. Supposing that we knew what a man is, he states, then we would have the criterion of truth which was sought, doubted, postulated or fruitfully exploited by all Greek philosophy. Aristotle believes that we do not know what man is. Do we possess the criterion of truth spoken of by Kierkegaard? For Aristotle, man is the being who, when asked a rational question, can give a rational answer. In this way, man becomes a responsible being, or moral subject. With respect to the criterion of truth, Aristotle wants us to remember that man is capable of responding to himself as well as to others. Aristotle learned well from his mentor Plato. Knowledge and morality must be identified as evolving from the same source. Both men realized they must defend the ideal of the absolute, the embodiment of universal truth.

Cassirer, like Aristotle, is cognizant of a philosophical debt when he says that man is a creature constantly in search of himself, a creature who, in every moment of his existence, must examine and scrutinize the conditions of his

Chapter One: The Meaning of Philosophy

existence.

The concept of man as creature is an important one for Aquinas. Regis senses its importance when he centers his position on this concept in his *Epistemology*. To know what a man is as a creature, he says, gives Thomistic epistemology its metaphysical context; but this context is not sufficient, for man is a particular creature and his imitation of God depends upon his own nature, since nature determines *esse*.

What makes man a particular creature? Cassirer makes a suggestion. It is only in our immediate intercourse with human beings, he says, that we have insight into the character of man. Kant would react by saying Cassirer does not carry this position far enough.

Kant contends that if it were possible to have so profound an insight into a man's mental character as shown by internal as well as external actions, as to know all its motives, even the smallest, and likewise all the external occasions that can influence them, we could calculate a man's conduct for the future with as great certainty as a lunar or solar eclipse, and maintain that the man is free.

By nature, man is motivated to learn. What makes a man a particular creature is his ability to learn how to learn; this he does together with other minds. The nature of his cognitive act makes him a particular creature. His concern is with infallible truth. Truth is an existent; his task is to discover and analyze cause in its relationship to truth. Man participates in what he learns; he judges the validity of his learning and places a value upon it. What he knows, he has experienced; experience makes reality meaningful to him. The origin of knowledge is the experience of reality.

It is the whole man who learns. It is by means of knowledge that man becomes something more than he was. This makes him something more than a being incidental to existence. As being, he is dependent upon being for existence. Existence implies the unification and integration of mind and content. He holds the most important position in the natural order. Existence is not external to his being; he is what exists; herein lies the being of his mind. He functions through the intermediary of objects; herein lies the motivation for learning. The task of his mind is to understand the objects in their relationship to his being. This is a natural habit, and it functions according to

Chapter One: The Meaning of Philosophy

an intellectual process. It is only man who can discover and formulate the laws of existence; it is a task reserved for the mind alone. It is man in relation to the objects of existence that brings him to the front in the development of epistemological thought.

Man the knower is man the existent. He is very much a part of what is yet to be known. The power of knowing is the power given him by the mind in relation to its objects. While he is but a part of substance, his mind makes it possible for him to relate parts and structure a vision of wholes; in the process, it is a matter of relating the self to what exists, as parts to be integrated to form new substance.

To learn, man must be at-one-with the object of learning. This is what it means to possess a synthetic consciousness. In other words, man is aware of himself as an intelligent being, capable of a consciousness which enables him to probe into the unknown and discover its mysteries. His potentiality as a learner resides in his mind; he knows his mind, as the totality of the self, must belong to the object of learning; this means there must be an identification with what is to be learned. In this way, man becomes a part of what he knows. This permits him to largely determine the contents of his universe. He reacts to what he knows; it is this reaction which enables him to internalize the object; what he does acts as a hypothesis to ascertain the meaningfulness of the confrontation, as well as its potentialities. This requires the use of the value judgment; it posits the belief that morality cannot be separated from the learning process.

This does not permit the learner to escape the fact that the natural order is also a determiner in the whole problem of epistemology. The natural order functions according to natural principles, all of which serve in the capacity of the starting point in the human process of intellection. Content-wise, these principles must be considered as working premises of cause. While they permit the mind to function freely, they serve as the sources of confrontation, the problems which must be analyzed and answered. Since the material of knowledge and its methodologies is a product of the natural order, it is therefore rational in nature. From these evolve man's motivation to learn. St. Thomas speaks of this movement when his theory of epistemology begins with man and moves to knowledge. From knowledge, it moves to its content or property, which is truth. Evolving from truth the mind moves to the characteristics of truth which are the specifics of certitude and potentiality.

Man is the knowing subject. The subject is the mind; it is the mind which knows and is the process of intellection, including the senses, memory and imagination. As the mind comes to know the natural order and its properties, it comes to know the self. It is at this point in the process of intellection that truth awaits verification. This process tells us that all thinking is reasoning, and reasoning, to be logical, must have premises and assumptions from which to reason. Man is the subject-matter, as well as the originator of, the material of knowledge. As originator, he is able to transcend the limitations of self. This is the same as saying that man is his own source of knowledge. First, he is a being, and secondly, an operant, functioning through the process of intellection and its procedural perspectives. The key which unlocks the mechanism of the process is the realization that the only way in which the object can be learned is for it to be internalized. It is at this point that consciousness assumes control in the learning process.

Man creates knowledge by understanding its content in relation to what he already knows.

The Learner as Knower

Kant was confused about the implications of experience when he tells us the knower participates in the formation of experience. This participation suggests a cleavage between the act of participation and the act of experience. Participation is experience; experience alone experiences experience. It is the knower, as the embodiment of what *is* for him, that experiences meaning.

To say the knower possesses knowledge is to say that he possesses the object. This does not imply that the being of the object is changed in this act of possession. This act is one of intellection, the object becoming an integral part of the essence of the mind. The object becomes united with the subject in the mind. Essentially, this is the cognitive act; it is the existential relationship between the object of knowing and the known. The essence of the object is the form which unites the knower and his object, but both "retain their existentiality."

The Learner as Philosopher

The true learner is a philosopher. There are nine reasons:

Chapter One: The Meaning of Philosophy

(1) He is, first and foremost, interested in cause. He knows all things have a beginning, and to know a thing is to know its first principles.

(2) He works by means of the intellective process. During the use of the process, he is always asking, what values am I able to derive from reason?

(3) He searches for the working principles which unite facts, parts with wholes. Identification and unification are two of his perspectives.

(4) He recognizes his need to understand the essence of matter, its nature as well as its potentiality.

(5) Mind, he knows, is more than matter; it is intelligible being. He raises the question, what could be more important for us to know than intelligible being?

(6) He understands the responsibilities of reflective thought and recognizes the limitations of observation. What, then, serves as objects of understanding? To answer this implies a concession to the demands of apprehension.

(7) The philosopher recognizes, suggests Blackstone, that the question of the meaning or cognitive significance of a statement is logically prior to the question of either the truth or falsity or the knowledge-status of that statement. Until one is reasonably clear about what is being claimed, one cannot possibly know what data are relevant to the confirming or disconfirming.

(8) Philosophers make cause and effect correlative.

(9) The true learner does not think in terms of mere actuality. His ideas, says Cassirier, cannot advance a single step without enlarging and even transcending the terms of the actual word.

Essentially, then, the true learner is a philosopher because he moves on the basic premise that nothing cannot be the cause of anything.

The Learner as Scientist

The true learner is a scientist. There are eight reasons why.

(1) He is, first and foremost, a theorist. He projects and tests theories. These theories are the result of observation, experimentation and perception. In looking for the past, he analyzes the present; the present he conceptualizes.

Chapter One: The Meaning of Philosophy

As he conceptualizes, his concern is with cause and its effects. For him, effect reflects cause. Here is where he locates his facts. He finds facts by reconstructing them and determining their dependency factors.

(2) Because one fact is dependent upon another fact for meaning and relevancy, for the scientist this implies harmony and number. His search is for the universal whole as the embodiment of truth.

(3) He is committed to the metaphysical content of knowledge.

(4) The direction his methodologies carry him is dependent upon the presuppositions he uses. His is the hypothesis method.

(5) He has an "intuition." This is not a guess, but rather a rapid analytical ratiocination of a synthetic insight aroused by the data already achieved. He tests it experimentally and experience shows him to be right or wrong, says Weigel and Madden.

(6) Reality for him is always on the empirical level. The theorist is the experimenter; theory without applicative value is meaningless. As theorist, he is a systematic and critical thinker. As experimenter, he experiences by perceiving data. He asks the question, what are the implications of this data?

(7) It is as scientist the learner enlarges knowledge. His explanations deal with the totality of phenomena. Totality implies dependencies among relationships; enlargement of knowledge comes through the recognition of necessary relationships. He not only records these relationships, but he conforms to them as well. He looks for patterns among existents.

(8) The true scientist, as a philosopher, makes no distinction between means and ends. He is "suspicious" of preconceived ideas; as a philosopher he questions whether an idea can be preconceived. Truth is his goal; truth is absolute but has relative values. To discover and then explore truth requires a mind philosophically oriented but empirically based.

Prime values constitute the essence of the lodestar which beckons the creative mind of the philosopher-scientist.

The Epistemological Premise

The epistemological premise is a proposition which holds within itself a high degree of accountability to other propositions.

Chapter One: The Meaning of Philosophy

For Descartes, the premise is an important factor in the theory of knowledge. It will be recalled that he insists we derive all human knowledge from premises whose truth is intuitively certain. This heavy responsibility which he places on intuition places him at a disadvantage when he analyzes his total epistemological schemata.

Ayer tells us that what Descartes was really trying to do was to base all knowledge on propositions which would be self-contradictory to deny. Descartes thought he had found such a proposition in "cognito," which must not here be understood in its ordinary sense of "I think," but rather as meaning "there is a thought now." Descartes was wrong because "non-cognito" would be self-contradictory only if it regarded itself; and this no significant proposition can do.

A significant proposition stands or falls upon its relationship to other propositions. It is the credibility factor which must be taken into account when propositions confirm or disconfirm each other. This relationship, says Russell, depends upon principles of inference, notably induction, which are never demonstrative, which yield only probabilities, and which, therefore, are not disproved when what they show to be probable does not happen.

We disagree with this position. Premises are always formulated in the construct of precepts. This is a necessary step in ascertaining the validity of a premise. Unless premises are explicit, their meaning will be subject to arguments which are not demonstrative and therefore not valid. This means that it is necessary to validate what I call step conclusions; that is, each conclusion evolves from the preceding premise. Here, in part, is one segment of Cartesian epistemology. It is necessary to depend upon premises and their intuitive powers for knowledge of conclusions. With respect to the question of inductive inference, it is a matter of believing, like Hume, that we move from instances of which we have experience to those of which we have none.

It is the premise which makes it possible for us to experience what has yet not been experienced. The premise leans heavily upon intuition for assistance. There are five "kinds" of premises which interest us. They are, first, the factual premises. Russell defines a factual premise as that which commands a greater or less degree of belief on its own account, independently of its relations to other propositions. This, of course, is contrary to our definition discussed above. While it is true that the premise does command a greater or less degree of belief on its own account, this is true only because of its relations to other propositions. Propositions are not entities, and when forced to become entities are no longer propositions. Second, memory premises. Earlier we stated that premises are always formulated in the construct of precepts. The reason for this is because every premise is a memory premise. We premise what we have experienced, and memory is our vehicle of recall basic to experience. This is another way of saying that every belief is caused; the cause is the precept. Russell would have us believe that a psychological premise may be defined as a belief which is not caused by any other belief or beliefs. Our answer to this paradox is found in our argument above. Third, the problematic premise. It is Popper who suggests that if we consider one of the premises, *i. e.,* either a universal law or an initial condition, as problematic, and the prognosis as something to be compared with the results of experience, then we speak of a test of the problematic premise. Fourth, the proximate premise. Price says that the proximate premise is an inductive generalization, and the ultimate premises are certain particular facts about the past, from which the generalization derives whatever probability it has, facts which are only accessible by means of memory. Fifth, a set of premises. Again, Russell addresses us. A set of premises is a minimum set in relation to a given body of propositions, if from the whole set, but not from any part of the set, all the given body of propositions can be deduced.

The Epistemological Question

Learning is a matter of studying problems. Education begins with the problem. Every problem is the object of knowledge. One characteristic of possessing knowledge is the ability to ask the right questions. As St. Thomas tells us, there is an art in asking the epistemological question.

It is an art tempered by an empirically based mind. The art is one filled with epistemological dangers. The phenomenologists have learned this time after time in their flirtation with idealism. Moreover, as they continue to taste their own delicacies the flavoring often bespeaks a touch of logical positivism. Dewey's instrumentalism, while it transcends the limits imposed upon it by James, those pragmatic in nature, fails because it does not place sufficient dependency upon presuppositions. Presuppositions refuse to permit the intellective process to over-simplify the relationships between propositions. Propositions evolve from the empirically structured question.

Chapter One: The Meaning of Philosophy

The empirically structured question is the one which probes into the underlying constructs of the presupposition. It wants to know if there is knowledge which is not experiential in nature. In addition, it wants to know if there is knowledge by cause. If so, does this imply that when the mind possesses knowledge, it has judged the validity of its essence? If so, what are the laws of condition? Is knowledge then, only a consequence of something else which happens?

In every epistemological question, there are presuppositions which the mind is forced to conceptualize. It is this process of conceptualization which structures the question. The question presupposes there is something to be known. The conceptualization process asks, what is already known about the unknown? What experience do we bring to the experimental process? What is inherent in the object and therefore inferential in its potentiality?

The epistemological question first asks these questions of itself before it moves on to take its place in the intellective process.

CHAPTER TWO
THE MEANING OF SCIENCE

We can apply the term science only to a body of knowledge, the certainty of which is apodictic. I define apodictic as that which is demonstrable. This can mean many things. For instance, is it possible to assume that science presupposes causality? What about the scientific method? Is causality assumed in its procedural technics? Does methodology presume to move from premises? Premises equivalent to cause? Is certainty to be found in what must always be considered process? Or, movement? Is it possible to demonstrate certainty from a meaningful inference? For instance, we ask, does science infer laws from particular facts? Are general laws inherent in premises? If so, what does this mean to an inference which is deductive in nature?

All these questions confront us when we attempt to define science. The problem is not whether science is possible, but how it is possible. This will be seen in the need to identify the possibility of science with the validity of synthetic judgments *a priori*. Whether or not we shall do this depends upon the direction taken in our definitive analysis of the mind of science.

The mind of science functions according to its presuppositions. They are as follows:

1. The perspective of science is determined by its search for order in phenomena.

2. The most important need of science is freedom of inquiry.

3. All dimensions of science are governed by the laws of subjective and objective necessity.

4. Because of its need for the freedom of inquiry, the spirit of science (which is independence of thought) expresses itself most forcibly in originality.

5. Science is without purpose until it possesses explanatory value systems.

6. The circumstance of science is the value condition from which its critical apparatus evolved.

Chapter Two: The Meaning of Science

7. The direction assumed by science and its methodology is determined by the nature of the essence of the universal.

8. It is the responsibility of science to establish principles of organization and unity: science implies knowledge organic in structure.

9. The means of science are brought into being by the attributes of empirically based insight.

10. The moral premises of science are based upon the needs of the human mind. Because of this, science is more than the means of acquiring knowledge. Because of its moral premises, science must concern itself with the consequences of its discoveries. Science is the mind of man at work on his problems.

11. Principles transcend facts in the same manner science enables the mind of values to transcend belief. The principles which underlie the methodologies of science require that it serve as the object of its own contemplative process.

12. Science, in its search for truth, finds it in meaning. While it is truth for which science searches, it is the potentiality of the explanatory power of truth which justifies the processes of science. The answers of science remain open to the apprehension and determination of yet more advanced degrees of truth. The quest of science is the quest of the human mind, namely, the need for truth. Intuited truth evolves from empirically based scientific truth. Science demands data as its first step toward the discovery of truth.

13. Science is the source of inspiration for the mind in its search for the bases of the intellective process. Science enables the mind to transcend its own limitations and identify with the value potential inherent in scientific knowledge. It is the human mind which must be held accountable for all decisions made in the methodological premises of science. Science achieves its prime and ultimate goal when the essence of the universal is actualized in the human mind; it strives to assist the mind to know by means of understanding cause; only in this way is it enabled to reason the essence of being. The mind has an irresistible need to know; science likewise has an irresistible need: to make it possible for the mind to know; it is science which seeks to provide the mind with a unified vision of experience. The goal of the human mind is to understand; this means developing its methodologies to the

Chapter Two: The Meaning of Science

degree that what is seen in fact provides the scientific base for determining potentiality. Science is not able to prove its object; when the mind experiences the meaning of the object, it is science which re-creates universals and particulars in the human mind. It is for the human mind (as well as by means of the human mind) that science determines the qualitative and quantitative relations between phenomena. It is mind using the empirically based insights of science which structure the competitive dialogs between hypotheses; sense perception is often imperfect; science is the means by which the mind functions as the intellective process to correct sense inadequacy.

14. It is reason which directs science in its search for, and discovery of, the unknown. Science reduces reason to a dependency upon First Cause and First Principles.

15. Science recognizes no absolute second causes; cause evolves from universals; cause extends itself as being through its essence. For science, cause is "the source of validated evidence."

16. Causal connections are realizable only in the eventuation of act.

17. It is causal laws "which provide the connectives between events." Causal laws imply that the natural order is self-explanatory.

18. Certitude is found only in the potentiality of probability.

19. To coordinate the data of consciousness is to empirically discipline the thought processes. The data of consciousness provides science with its first experience of knowing.

20. Science does not move in the demand-state of finality; rather, its momentum is derived from the on-going search for the potentiality of potentiality. Science is the architect of the potentiality of fact.

21. Science bases its methodologies on principles which evolve from First Cause. It is the principle of causality which enables science to be predictive. It is science and its methodologies which make it possible for the intellect to actualize its perspectives and intentions.

22. The value system of science is predicated on the value conditions accepted by the human mind.

23. Science is dependent upon value and proportion in the construct of

Chapter Two: The Meaning of Science

any unity; to determine relationships within a whole is to structure principles of integration, thereby enabling the mind to relate parts with parts, and parts to the whole.

24. It is the value condition which permits science to function through its methodologies. Science provides the data foundation out of which value conditions evolve.

25. The predictive abilities of science are controlled by its validating methodologies.

26. Phenomena is the object of science. The relationships which exist between natural phenomena are explained only by the principles which identify natural phenomena and cause.

27. In order for science to explain, it must first experience meaning. Scientific explanation becomes, in essence, the value judgment. Science explains the unknown by the known.

28. It is within the mind of scientific determinism that historical knowledge gains its impetus in the intellective process. The determinism characteristic of all science is metaphysical as well as methodological.

29. To discover the hidden potential in a fact is the goal of the organizational qualities of the methodological structure of science. In the process of correlating facts, science is enabled to see the potentiality of those facts. For science, an indifferent fact is nonexistent. Science controls its facts through the systematization and organization of their causal principles. It is science which classifies the facts of experience and incorporates them into the structure of its methodologies.

30. Science values the thought itself as much as the thought process; in the same way it values the discovery and its potentialities as much as the structuring of methodologies which made the discovery possible. Science provides thought with its organizational patterns. Mode of thought for science is its analysis and summary of the fact. Science orders thought and patterns it for new direction.

31. To interpret universals and particulars, science uses transcendental thought; to experience perceptually interpretative principles is to have localized cause and its assumptions.

Chapter Two: The Meaning of Science

32. Scientific theories are judged only by standards of objective and subjective validity; they are the approximations of what is true.

33. Theoretical speculation evolves from the validation process which is an integral part of every theory test.

34. The essence of the real is a quality of the ultimate. Science endeavors to discover a reality which is self sufficient; that is, in its ultimate form. When science synthesizes knowledge, the real is found in unity. The real is fully realizable only in its potentiality.

35. Science is both inductive and deductive in its methodologies. In the solution of its problems, science depends upon the construct of new methodic theories in order to experience working principles.

36. Cosmology is theory of knowledge in the same manner cosmology is science.

37. A scientific law is a comprehensive whole; the correlation of validated facts serve as causal principles.

38. It is the scientific concept which describes form in matter; it is the process of conceptualization which does not permit form to degenerate and become formulae. Science is the mind of the connectives of concepts. To determine the potentiality of the concept is to actualize the logicality of fact. It is the concept which dissects the fact, searching for the components of its structure; it is science which designs the concept. To unify the object of conceptualization is to experience the fact inherent in its potentiality.

39. The need to recognize rationality in nature is one of the greatest needs of the mind of science.

40. Logic is a built-in construct of science.

41. Before it is possible for science to harmonize beliefs, the mind must have faced up to the need for the expiation of attitudes.

42. Science is the integrator and unifier of all dimensions of human experience. Experience is the test of the concept; science is the systematization of the inherent structure of the process of conceptualization, the means by which experience fuses experience into itself.

43. Abstraction, as a method of science, is the only means by which the

Chapter Two: The Meaning of Science

quality of essence (as reality) can be actualized.

44. Necessity is actualized by experience; necessity is the embodiment of reason, the understanding of which is experienced by intelligible modes of thought.

45. All epistemology is scientific in nature.

46. The position that the physical universe is ruled by chance is obsolete.

47. Science is evolutionary in its process of analysis. Science does not establish laws; rather, it discovers them. Moreover, its aim is to discover the implicative value meaning inherent in every law.

48. The nature of being is structured by its necessities; it is these immanent qualities which are of prime concern to science.

49. Every conclusion is inherent in its principles. It is impossible to finalize knowledge until its science actualizes ultimates.

Many aims have become readily apparent in our listing of the presuppositions of science. It will be helpful to draw certain conclusions at this point.

Science does not operate from an inflexible base; it is a viable thing. Its methodologies, governed by ideas, are continually evolving, changing the perspective of the intellective process. In its search for truth, its predictive sense is constantly moving to the front, recognizing the need, as du Noüy suggests,

> to classify our knowledge and to establish relations between observable phenomena in order to be able to predict the future in a certain measure and to explain the sequence of phenomena in relation to ourselves. These relations are called laws, and when no exceptions are known they become scientific principles. Laws or principles always rest on measurements, that is to say relations: relation of the quantity measured to an arbitrary quantity taken as a unit.

Whenever the mind works with relationship, it is confronted by the need for an intellectual activity which is creative; it is within that creative activity that purposive explanations are to be found. Here is the source of the scientific idea. It means that a standard of judgment has been established as a

Chapter Two: The Meaning of Science

working base, but the intellective process, because it runs on epistemological energy, strives to move beyond its premises. Here is the point at which scientific ideas come into being. These are the ideas which bring understanding of an object and the sense experience of its potentiality.

Abstract thought is creative thought, expressing itself by means of the process of conceptualization. It is thought as experience which penetrates reality and expands it. This is the responsibility of conceptualization and its processes.

CHAPTER THREE
THE MEANING OF KNOWLEDGE

From among all epistemologists, St. Thomas alone speaks of a respect for the nature of the pre-eminent life that is knowledge. This attitude characterizes his system of epistemology in which he reminds us that our knowledge of truth and its existence parallels our knowledge of the nature of the intellect.

This respect for knowledge and its material, and the mind and its processes, provides the key to the pivot of his epistemological theory, and suggests a starting point for defining knowledge. This starting point is a simple one, clear in its lines: knowledge is totally dependent on the object, and the object is totally independent of the knowledge the mind may possess of it. This means there is an intimate contact between subject and object, the object existing, awaiting the action of the intellective process, but while waiting, providing revelatory directives for the mind to use. It is the object which provides the opportunity for the mind to experience "the beatific vision" of what the object can come to mean in the mind.

Knowledge is experience; it begins with, and continues as the mind experiences the essence of an object. The object, at first, exists as the unknown, but at the point of the intimate contact, the fact of confrontation brings with it revelatory dimensions of the object's existence. With confrontation, the mind is awakened to the potential inherent in the object and the search for understanding (meaning) begins. To experience meaning is to actualize the object, ultimately making it an integral part of the subject itself. This is what makes knowledge an immanent activity.

Knowledge, then, is an awareness of the object confronting the mind, and a consciousness of the meaning inherent in the object. Both subject and object are realities, in the same way modes and conclusions drawn in thought as ideas are real. It is the dialog between the qualities of the mind and the qualities of all other existence which produces knowledge. It is the generation

Chapter Three: The Meaning of Knowledge

of ideas by the mind, by what it already possesses as essence, and the generation of ideas by the mind in relation to external objects, which provide the material upon which the mind works.

Knowledge does not exist until the mind experiences its material, actualizing its object. To experience the material of knowledge is to perceive the dependency connectives between subject and object and the operational consequences derived from the confrontation. Here, says Guzie, is the union of knower and his object in an immanent act, but, "for, the object known, while intentionally immanent, is existentially other than the knower."

The mind of knowledge functions according to its presuppositions. They are as follows:

1. Knowledge is knowledge of our self-consciousness.

2. The qualification of knowledge is by ideas.

3. To quantify knowledge is to develop concepts for the prime purpose of multiplying the objects inherent in the essence of the material of knowledge.

4. Thought without interpretation is as mind without knowledge. Knowledge is the thought of the knowable object expressing itself by means of the revelatory powers of its intrinsic structure. Transcendental thought makes it possible for empirical truth to be experienced. Knowledge is the mode of thought developed by the intellective process as it experiences the essence of an object. Critical reflective thought is a means used by the mind in its need to possess knowledge.

5. While knowledge may be a cognition of appearance, the actualization of essence makes depth of knowledge possible. To possess knowledge is to possess the ability to express the meaning of its essence. One means by which knowledge reveals its essence is by sense impression, a feed-back to the mind. While knowledge is ultimate, its essence is analyzable. To possess knowledge is impossible for the mind unable to conceptualize. Knowledge is neither copy nor reproduction; its essence produces the real. The basic component in the essence of knowledge is the proposition with its inferences. To perceive knowledge is to conceptualize its material; to conceptualize knowledge is to perceive the structure of its essence. To possess knowledge is to know essence. To determine the essence of knowledge is to vitalize the process of revelatory construction. Knowledge combines the constructs of its essence to

Chapter Three: The Meaning of Knowledge

add to its dimensions.

6. First principles serve as the source of all knowledge.

7. To experience meaning is to interiorize being, the nature of knowledge. Multiplicity in proposition is reduced to unity only when the mind experiences the totality of meaning. Knowledge, as the consciousness of meaning, is the presupposition intuited in all meaning. All meaning is contextual; this means that knowledge is the resultant of the cognitive experience of the mind actualizing its object. To discover meaning is to qualify the experiential value inherent in the object, as the material of knowledge. Meaning is experienced when cause becomes means, and effects are actualized in means. Knowledge without meaning is no longer knowledge; it is coextensive with experienced meaning. When knowledge becomes identical with essence, meaning is realized.

8. Knowledge begins with causal abstractions.

9. There is a cognitive intentionality inherent in the data of all knowledge.

10. Knowledge integrates and unifies the thinking man with his confrontations.

11. Knowledge is the actualization of the real; it is the realization of the essence of the real. Knowledge reveals the presuppositions of reality. While all knowledge is real, its task is to disclose the nature of reality. The pattern of reality is knowledge expressed by means of the experience of the knower. Knowledge, the product of selective thought and the possession of the qualities of reality, is the perceptive experiential enfoldment of the real, the embodiment of an objectified reality. Reality is sensible in the same manner mind experiences meaning.

12. Knowledge is the actualization of experience; this is the starting point of the intellective process. Experience is neither past nor future; within each proposition of knowledge lies the conditions necessary for its existence as well as the potentiality necessary for its actualization. Further experience serves as the check on the interpretative abilities of the mind. There is no knowledge independent of experience; knowledge destroys the false conception that connectors exist between experiences. There is no "between" experiences; knowledge is experience; its essence is a fused one. Knowledge makes it possible for the mind to objectify experience in preparation for

Chapter Three: The Meaning of Knowledge

further experience, and evolves from the mind experiencing the relations among experience. Principles serve as the data of experience.

13. When the mind experiences its object, the antecedents of the object are realized as existentially knowable; when mind penetrates its object, it experiences, by thought, the nature of essence. Inherent within knowledge are the rules which govern and direct the mind in its discovery of essence. In knowing, the mind reasons its object and experiences its essence. Knowledge is the cognitive reaction of the mind to the confrontation encountered between subject and object. The mind conscious of its essence is a mind using its knowledge to interpret its data. Knowledge is non-existent as long as the mind is not conscious of its relationship to an object. Knowledge, as the content of the reflective power of the mind, is the transparency factor in the mind's ability to analyze and interpret its object. The mind guards against the relativity of perception by means of its cognitive sense. The mind knows itself by means of the knowledge which it possesses of its essence; knowledge is the definition of the essence of the mind.

14. Depth in knowledge is qualitative. Knowledge is experienced when the mind employs, by means of the intellective process, the qualities of its essence. The quality of knowledge is found only in its power for conceptualization. Knowledge is knowledge of quality. As an existent, the concern of knowledge is with the essence of its qualities.

15. The knowledge contained in words is realizable when, as symbols, they provide the incentive for reaction. All knowledge is expressed in words; this does not mean that knowledge is only of words.

16. While knowledge is fact, its certitude is the reality of its existence.

17. Knowledge presupposes a knowledge of knowledge. To possess knowledge is to possess an understanding of its assumptions.

18. The knowledge of an idea is to possess a knowledge of the source of the idea. While ideas evolve from ideas, this does not presuppose a reduplication of knowledge; knowledge implies an understanding of the essence of an idea in relation to another idea. To possess knowledge is to possess the ability to trace the history of an idea from its inception to its actualization.

19. Knowledge is never copy; it is the osmotic process of complete

Chapter Three: The Meaning of Knowledge

identification.

20. Verification of knowledge is dependent upon the nature of the historical present in experience.

21. To possess knowledge is to have interpreted the essence of its material.

22. As act of subject, knowledge as object, becomes its subject.

23. To perceive an object is to possess a knowledge of its essence. Knowledge is gained when the knower identifies experientially with the object. All knowledge is historic in nature; the historical process is inherent in the intellective process, therefore, within the nature of the object itself. Every object, as the material of knowledge, expresses its potentiality in the act of thought. The object of knowledge serves to fulfill the potential mind stance of the subject. Certain knowledge of an object is the realization that its essence cannot be doubted. Knowledge, as what is experienced of an object, is dependent upon the perceptive abilities of the mind. While object exists independently of the subject (such independence is necessary if the mind is to perceive it) it is the qualities of the object which become identical with the subject.

24. Knowledge of what is false has been so proven because of the empirical premises of the known; knowledge is the structuring of premise and inference.

25. Methodology is the process chosen by the mind to perfect the knowledge of its essence.

26. The potentiality of knowledge is resident in its ability to predict the evolutionary perspectives of its ideas; it is the applicative idea which proceeds from meaning. Knowledge results when cause becomes means and effects become the consequences of an object actualized for its potentiality. Knowledge is what is, and changes its nature and meaning only when its potentiality is actualized.

27. Knowledge knows no boundaries.

28. The mind alone is able to unify the propositions of knowledge.

29. The language of knowledge is the verbalization of meaning.

Chapter Three: The Meaning of Knowledge

30. The intellect functions in the state of becoming; when knowledge is possessed, the intellect moves from potentiality to actuality.

31. All knowledge is sensible; this means it has meaning for the mind, the sensate quality of being.

32. Truth ontologizes the being of knowledge in its revelatory powers. The truth of knowledge is identical to the being of its essence. Truth is realizable only as the mind actualizes the real and determines its potentiality by means of the material of knowledge; possessed truth is certain meaning.

33. The being of knowledge is identical with the truth of its material. Knowledge is the realization of one's own being, the study of personal essence. It is the objective order in being which structures the object, making it identifiable by the intellective process, and subject to analysis as the essence of the reality of knowledge. All knowledge is dependent upon the ability of the mind to cognitively reflect upon the correlatives in the structure of being; the relation of knowledge to being is the relation of parts to the whole.

34. Form is the stricture in the perceptive process of intellection on its movement toward the discovery of the potentiality of the material of knowledge. Form in knowledge is determined by the structure of its particulars and qualified by the nature of the universal. The forms of knowledge are the categories structured and devised by the relationship between subject and object.

35. The directive inherent in the cognitive act is dependent upon the nature of the ability of the mind to experience its object.

36. All knowledge possesses a cognitive order, the determinant of absolute value.

37. Knowledge is an absolute with relative values.

38. The intellective process synthesizes the conceptual power of the material of knowledge. Conjecture as to the potentiality of the material of knowledge is an integral part of the perspective of the intellective process. Characteristic of all material of knowledge is an intrinsic unity implied within the material of knowledge as the objective judgment. There is a logical structure to the material of knowledge, an order to quantify components in its essence. To analyze the material of knowledge is to depend upon the

Chapter Three: The Meaning of Knowledge

directives inherent in the source of the object of knowing. It is the data of the material of knowledge which is the essence of the mind; knowledge is the reality of its material.

39. Knowledge is the resultant of communication, the reaction to propositions.

40. Knowledge arises from inquiry, the action of which constitutes its material.

41. All knowledge is ultimately reduced to belief. Without the belief inherent in faith, knowledge cannot exist. Belief is a resultant of the mind's ability to conceptualize truth.

42. Knowledge results when there has been the correlation of concepts to form a new concept.

43. All knowledge is founded on an inherent objectivity, the nature of which is based on the experiential qualities encountered in the process of conceptualization.

44. The principle of knowledge is governed by the mode of thought structured by the knower.

45. Responsibility inherent in the nature of knowledge is evidenced by its recognition of the dependency needs of particulars in relation to the universal; inherent in knowledge is the universal.

46. The nature of knowledge is resident in the infallibility of its truth, and is characterized by its symbolical inferences.

47. All knowledge is assimilative in nature.

48. Knowledge is the resultant of: (a) the evolutionary intellective process which has as its own the identification of object with subject; (b) the mind's interpretative ability to experience the given; (c) the reasoning powers of the intellective process. Knowledge is more than receptivity; it is the resultant of the mind's ability to experience its object. As a resultant, knowledge is the synthesis of experimental thought and the cognitive act.

49. Knowledge, as the consciousness of the essence of existence and the embodiment of the idea of being, is the essence of consciousness. Knowledge, as the experience of meaning, is dependent upon knowledge as the experience

Chapter Three: The Meaning of Knowledge

of consciousness.

50. Knowledge is the apprehension of: (a) the correlatives inherent in the relationship between existence and essence; (b) the factual base of being; (c) the essence of reality. The relationship which portends mere acquaintance, in turn, portends low degrees in the apprehension of knowledge.

51. While knowledge is the appropriation of the given, it transcends the given as the mind objectifies its being.

52. The significance of knowledge is found in the interpretational qualities of the mind.

53. It is the intellective process which formulates structure in knowledge. The structure of knowledge is dependent upon its perceptive abilities in relation to the directives inherent in form.

54. Knowledge evolves when the mind experiences cause and the correlative system of meanings delineate the presuppositions of first principles. To possess knowledge is to understand its cause; its existence depends upon the experiential activity of the mind in relation to intentional sources. Knowledge is conditioned upon the ability of the mind to experience the presuppositions inherent in cause.

55. The function of knowledge is actualized only by reflective thought, the assumptive aim of reason.

56. Knowledge is a fact when the meaning of the object of knowing is experienced by the knower.

57. Knowledge is non-existent until the intellective process incorporates within its own being the perspective of relational logic.

58. To comprehend intuitively is to understand the objective judgment. The intuitive powers of knowledge reside in the intellective process.

59. Perception is the intellective organizer of the material of knowledge.

60. Existence is the presupposition of knowledge; it is the correlate of essence and determines the condition of what is known.

61. Of utmost concern to knowledge is its responsibility to discern the nature of the change affecting the correlations among its working hypothesis.

Chapter Three: The Meaning of Knowledge

62. The intellective process is without direction until the criterial of knowledge has been determined. The only criterion of knowledge acceptable to the mind is a logical statement.

63. The value of knowledge lies in its intrinsic potentiality, and in the fact that its essence is not an end in itself.

Considering the implications of the assumptions listed above, it is evident there are a number of "problem areas" in the science of epistemology which must be looked at.

Since it is our basic contention that knowledge is the experience of meaning, and experience is the existential component of the human mind, to experience meaning is to possess certainty of what exists.

The act of knowledge is existential in moment; this means that as an act is completed it functions as an activity and its essence is that of movement. The "in moment" factor is when the mind assimilates its object; it is *when* the mind knows. This is the existential moment in epistemology; it is when mind attains, by assimilation, being. It is the moment when the mind experiences meaning, and the act of judgment has been completed.

Actual knowledge is knowledge which has been experienced via its intended meaning. This means the mind has realized its existence as real, and the epistemological consciousness of the mind has functioned by means of the intellective process.

The mind is unable to function from nothing, or with nothing. There is movement only in confrontation, that is, in the relationship between subject and object. The same is true for knowledge. Popper tells us that knowledge cannot start from nothing, the tabula rasa, nor yet from observation. The advance of knowledge consists, he says, mainly in the modification of earlier knowledge.

It is possible that alleged knowledge is merely unsubstantiated belief.

To analyze knowledge is to experience the implicative values inherent in evidence. The implication itself is one of knowing being. To know being is to be aware of the potentialities resident in an epistemological perspective, and possess the necessary determinants for the actualization of truth.

What is the relationship of knowledge to reality? Is not the question, in

Chapter Three: The Meaning of Knowledge

itself, a paradox? Is it possible to make a distinction? In epistemology, is the proposition applied to reality? Again, a paradox. Rather, is this not the problem? What epistemological refinements make it possible for the intellective process to analytically deduce propositions from premises and concepts? What determines validity for a given proposition?

Polanyi does not hesitate to remind us that the conceptual framework of applicable knowledge is different from that of pure knowledge. Moreover, he says, it is determined primarily in terms of the successful performances to which such knowledge is relevant... the suitability of an object... is an observable property, but it can be observed only within the framework defined by the performance it is supposed to serve.

Is it possible for knowledge to exist which is logically prior to experience? That is, independent of experience? If so, what position does this place the mind in the cognitive act? If so, what type of definition does this force upon experience? What implications does it hold for universal principles? For empirical particulars? Perhaps this suggests that *a priori* knowledge is only analytical in nature? If this is true, would it not force empirical knowledge into the pale of mere probability?

The data resident in the working hypothesis is suggesting a certainty; this is what serves as the premise upon which the cognitive act proceeds. It is the means chosen by the mind to articulate its knowledge.

Knowledge does not exist unless it is assimilative in nature; the controlling factors here involve the ability of the mind for conceptualization, and the empirical dimensions of the intellective process.

Scheffler holds that the attributions of knowledge are not, in typical cases, simply descriptive of bodies of lore or types of experience; they experience our standards, ideals, and tastes as to the scope and proper conduct of the cognitive acts. They reflect, for example, conceptions of truth and evidence, estimates of the possibilities of secure belief, and our preferences among alternative strategies of investigation. To describe someone as knowing, he says, is as much to appraise and approve as it is to report. Correspondingly, education is concerned to transmit not only what we know, but our manner of knowing, that is, our approved standards of competence in performance, in inquiry, and in intellectual criticism.

Chapter Three: The Meaning of Knowledge

Authority for the validation of knowledge resides in cause as first principles. While reason is a methodology, its data justifies its aim existence as the material of knowledge. It is source which provides the authoritative criteria so necessary in the cognitive act.

There is nothing uncertain about the boundaries of knowledge; there are none. Discovery prepares the mind for discovery; the intellective process demands constant movement and progression. In this sense, an idea makes it possible for another idea to be brought into being. There are no limits within these conditions. Cassirer addresses himself to this when he says that all the branches of knowledge presuppose a higher unity where all meet and so are members of an organism that possess a concrete reality.

It has often been suggested that knowledge by causes

can be of two types, because there are two modes of causality, intrinsic and extrinsic. The intrinsic mode is subdivided into matter and form in material things considered in the abstract, and into potency and act when these same things are considered as being. The extrinsic mode is sub-divided into efficiency and finality. Knowledge that grasps reality in its intrinsic causes is knowledge by apprehension; whereas the grasp of extrinsic causes depends upon reasoning, a complex act whose object includes the complexity of relations between cause and effect. (Regis)

To say that things are intelligible is to imply they possess the potentiality for meaningfulness. To insure intelligibility as well as meaningfulness calls for an understanding of cause as first principles of knowledge. Cause is an active agent in the intellective process; it is the source of the operational perspective of the cognitive act.

We raise two questions: (1) how does the mind inquire into the premises upon which certitude rests? and (2) what happens to the mind when it possesses certain knowledge?

Certainty as a concept always confronts us with the question of doubt. The master of this problem is Descartes. He makes every attempt to establish certainty in knowledge by means of the reflexive method. One can doubt the existence of the external world and even of his own body, he says. They may be objects of an illusion or of a dream, or appearances produced by an evil

Chapter Three: The Meaning of Knowledge

spirit. But one cannot doubt that he doubts Und therefore that he thinks) without contradiction. The proposition "I think" is supposed to be undeniable on principle, since it is apparently presupposed through its denial. It may be observed that the Cartesian argument presupposes the validity of memory, so that it cannot lay claim to absolute certainty. One can always doubt that he doubted. If it is not possible to doubt that one is doubting at a given moment, as a matter of psychological fact, it is also true that it is not possible to affirm the doubting process at the same time. Once the doubting experience is over, it is possible to doubt that it ever happened. (Farber)

Our questions raised above, as well as those which confront us in Descartes position, will require our attention at every point in our analysis of epistemological theory.

If we are to believe Plato, the implications of his position are far-reaching for even the most highly structured idealist. Human knowledge, he says, has an immaterial character. The object of this knowledge is outer reality. This, too, must be immaterial.

What, then, makes reality real? Of what is the essence of the material of knowledge?

What is the starting point of complete knowledge? Aristotle says: omnis cognitio nostra a sensu incipit. Not at all. Complete knowledge does not start from sensory perception, and sensory perception does not cause "the first awakening of consciousness." We cannot perceive without benefit of a highly developed sense of consciousness. Is this what Aristotle really meant?

What determines our conception of knowledge? Without question, what we know is in relation to what is already known, and how we know is in relation to learning models already structured by the mind. The mind functions experientially; this means with what it has to work; it functions upon and through its essence. Ideas comprise the sum of essence; the quality of the idea in relation to quality in other ideas provides the interaction underlying the intellective process. It is this activity which provides the hypothesis inherent in every intellectual act with a conception of meaning. To conceive meaning is to experience knowledge. Both factors are necessary in our determinative process which alone culminates in a conception of knowledge. To determine a conception of knowledge is to experience an

Chapter Three: The Meaning of Knowledge

intellectual act.

With the attainment of conceptual knowledge, the mind is enabled to conceptualize. A paradox? No. It is a matter of determining relationships. For knowledge to be attained, the mind finds meaning in its object; for instance, meaning is found in matter; thus, there is a relationship to matter. To find meaning implies the mind possesses its object; to do this, it has to transcend mere representation and conceptualize being. Conceptual knowledge means the mind understands the relation of meaning to its object. True, it is a matter of abstraction, but then, this is characteristic of all processes of conceptualization. It is conceptual knowledge which makes of all reality common.

The primary condition for knowledge is consciousness. This means, in order to learn, the mind must be able to experience meaning conscious of intention as well as implications of the object. Mind is the only reality which can experience meaning in what exists.

While knowledge is what is possessed by the mind, its original existence was independent of the mind. Essence exists outside the mind until experience brings it within the mind via the meaning it portends. The content of knowledge is experienced reality. There can be no knowledge without its content.

We cannot determine criteria until we have answered the question, what is the nature of reality? This requires the mind to metaphysically conceptualize the essence of the real. All this is quite contrary to Dewey's thinking. He would have us believe the criterion of knowledge lies in the method used to secure consequences. This is true, in part. It also lies in metaphysical conceptions of the nature of the real. This does not place all emphasis on subject, or, in the Aristotelian stance, believe that the subject exercises a function in the act of knowledge which is exclusively proper to itself. Here we do not agree with his use of the word *exclusively*. Finality has a goal, and for knowledge, the relationship between subject and object is the content of the experience; the intention of the real expresses itself in the meaning which has been understood.

What are the problem areas in an attempt to answer the question, what is knowledge? We raise them as questions.

Chapter Three: The Meaning of Knowledge

1. What makes it possible to define knowledge in a way in which the definition serves as a "vision of unity"?

2. What is the "inner dynamism" of the knowing subject: Is it knowledge?

3. What is the being of knowledge?

4. Is the search for knowledge the search for essence?

5. How does definition express essence?

6. What is the relationship between the knower and reality?

7. Is reality the material of knowledge?

8. What are the characteristics of the material of knowledge?

9. Is truth existential property of knowledge?

10. In what ways does knowledge confront reflection?

11. Is the substance of knowledge absolute? Does it possess cause?

12. What is the efficient principle of knowledge?

13. Is cause and source of knowledge to be considered identical?

14. The nature of knowledge, does it refer only to the human mind?

15. What are the objects which characterize knowledge?

Reviewing the above questions in a sense forces us to consider, as first response, the implications of discursive knowledge. It is Dewey who provides us with a thought setting on the subject. Discursive knowledge, that which involved reflection, he says, must always be referred for its validation back to what is immediately known. It cannot bring its credentials with it and test its results in the very process of reaching them. There is postulated identity implicit or explicit of the results of inference with things known without inference. Making the identity explicit constitutes proof.

This raises yet another question. Is it possible for a duality of knowledge to exist? Is the theory of knowledge predicated on these assumptions: (1) consciousness makes it possible for knowledge to be possessed; and (2) to conceptualize is to experience meaning.

Thought is the working base of all experience; experience is the

Chapter Three: The Meaning of Knowledge

embodiment of consciousness.

To delineate problem areas in empirical knowledge, it is necessary to look at its premises; these number thirteen.

1. Empirical knowledge affirms pure perceptive propositions. (Russell)

2. Empirical knowledge requires premises asserting matters of fact. (Russell)

3. Empirical knowledge defines basic propositions as those of its logically indemonstrable propositions which are themselves empirical, *i.e.,* assert some temporal occurrence. (Russell)

4. Empirical knowledge consists of indirections from a number of more or less similar experiences. (Russell)

5. Empirical knowledge insists there is *always* an empirical factor in knowledge, even the knowledge of the *a priori*. (Weigel and Madden)

6. Empirical knowledge expresses its perfect form through the categories in the judgment where the object indicated receives its meaning in the predicate of judicial affirmation. (Weigel and Madden)

7. Empirical knowledge gives an existence of otherness. Except through empirical knowledge, the mind cannot know the otherly existence. Consciousness cannot give it. (Weigel and Madden)

8. Empirical knowledge, by categories, is essentially different from consciousness which is pure awareness without categories. Both may be called empirical because they entail experience, but they are different in their reaction to the experimented. Both are intellectual, but in empirical knowledge a process is entailed which must include the material aspects of man. A pure spirit could not achieve knowledge by empirical discovery. (Weigel and Madden)

9. Empirical knowledge eventually goes back to knowledge of empirical particulars. Generalizations have their ground in the coincidence of such particulars. Knowledge of the particular functions also as the basis of the applicability of general principles which are not empirical but *a priori*. Knowledge of the particular is rooted in immediate experience. (Lewis)

10. Empirical knowledge is exclusively a knowledge of probabilities, the

Chapter Three: The Meaning of Knowledge

validity of it in general depends upon the validity of induction and probability-judgment. (Lewis)

11. Empirical knowledge contrasts itself with judgment of pure reason, the axioms, principles, and categories of reason. (Watkin).

12. Empirical knowledge recognizes the principle of causality. (Cassirer)

13. Empirical knowledge is based on a logical doctrine concerning the distinction between analytic propositions, synthetic propositions, and metaphysical verbiage. (Ayer)

Maritain speaks of empiriometric knowledge as that knowledge which resolves its concepts not in being, but exclusively in the measurable, and which man perceives that everything in the physical world cannot be strictly measured.

The essence of knowledge we are equating with the material of knowledge; yet, this position may confuse the epistemologically oriented mind unless we think of essence in the same vein as Kant, that is, the essence of knowledge as synthesis. Synthesis bespeaks a totality, either as an existent, purely in the realm of the potential. Even this stance does not force us to say that the essence of knowledge lies primarily in intuition. It may. Only, however, if we allow the intuition to be directed by the cognitive process. Intuition is much more than Kant would have us believe when he says intuition takes place only insofar as the object is given to us.

It is the responsibility of existential knowledge to raise questions about its own being. This it does by means of methodological inquiry, using the value judgment to form its beliefs about means. Its concern is with the will, the source of motivation for the intellect. The will serves as the dominant principle as well as the source of epistemological energy as the mind moves, by degrees, on the scale of apprehension toward the experiencing of meaning.

The existence of knowledge is the ability of the mind to interiorize its essence or material.

In what way can we raise questions about knowledge unless we understand the implicative values inherent in the fact of knowledge? Does this force us to begin with knowledge as a given? To do so would insist we think of the intellective process as the embodiment of a knowledge in order to

Chapter Three: The Meaning of Knowledge

experience knowledge. Our question then, is, is knowledge a given?

What implications are there in the foregoing question which might lead us to agree with Carnap that to gain factual knowledge a non-logical procedure is always necessary? Would not such a position force us to ask, what are the criteria for factual knowledge? Blackstone seems to feel he has the answer. Factual knowledge, he says, is always informative about the world. K includes descriptions and explanations of the phenomena of nature. It is inferential and testable; however, the testing procedures can at best render factual inferences highly probable, never completely certain. Even if the present available evidence completely support a given factual belief, there is always the possibility that some important data have overlooked, and the further possibility that future experience will provide confirming data.

Guzie approaches the problem by saying that factual knowledge is heavily sensory. Of course it is; all knowledge is sensory; it is the only operant setting from which the mind can function. Even the most abstract idea possesses a sensory base. Guzie continues. The intellect, he would have us believe (though we do not) does little more than assent to the truth of the fact represented (or questionable word) in phantasms. This is not to say that factual knowledge is unimportant. Though the intellectual content of an act of assent to concrete facts is minimal, factual knowledge supplies the foundation for any higher type of cognition. It is here, he says, that the mind gradually builds up a store of phantasms which will be instruments for future intellectual knowledge.

We may say, then that Steenberghen is correct in his assumption that the finality of knowledge is the datum of consciousness as well as a fact.

The central point in the functional view of knowledge, Cassirer says, is in the relation of thought to object. Since we are inferring problems and areas for further thought, we take the liberty of exchanging the propositions of Cassirer for questions. When is the object to be treated as a given fact as well as a problem? When does the object serve as the goal of knowledge, and not as its starting point? What constitutes the realm of its own operations? Is knowledge built up by stages? As the process advances, does the object become more and more sharply designated? Do we progress from general to the particular, abstract to concrete determinations, and then try to show how the latter presuppose the former and are based upon them?

Chapter Three: The Meaning of Knowledge

Steenberghen responds. Growth in knowledge, he says, is an essential element in the development of man's personality as well as, on the level of society, of human civilization. The educated man strives not only to extend his store of knowledge, but also to organize and evaluate the data of popular knowledge. It is this effort which gives rise to scientific life. In his desire for knowledge man thus seeks an ideal of unity. Incapable of a unique intuitive act that would satisfy his whole appetite for knowledge, he admits that human knowledge can arrive at unity only through the unity of a synthesis.

There is an ordered wholeness in all existence. The mind, as an existent and as the knowing power, strives to identify with this ordered wholeness, thereby actualizing its material. Is this the sum and substance, then, of the cognitive act?

Dewey locates our problem for us. He says that it has often been assumed that higher education must be supplied by pure thought. Now, it is taken for granted that thought, while indispensable to knowledge of natural existence, can never in itself, provide knowledge. Observation is indispensable both to provide authentic materials to work upon and to test and verify the conclusion reached by theoretical considerations. A specific kind of experience is indispensable to science instead of all experience setting a limit to the possibility of true science.

The problem is whether or not observation has the ability to provide what Dewey demands; perhaps it is to perception we must turn to meet these requirements. Moreover, there appears to be a problem of historicity involved.

If we agree with Mannheim that all historical knowledge is relational knowledge, then we are faced with the task of discriminating between what is true and what is false in such knowledge.

We raise only one question here. The product of thought, is this the only means at our disposal for identifying knowledge?

Ideal knowledge exists when the mind as subject experiences the object; in such experience the object as the material of knowledge is fused in the subject. We are interested, of course, in the problem of epistemological fusion. It is identical with the cognitive act?

Scheffler structures our question: what about the present fact itself? Rejecting infallible knowledge of causal connections, some have affirmed,

Chapter Three: The Meaning of Knowledge

while others have denied, that a special sort of certainty attaches to mere empirical description. Recall that the main brunt of Hume's argument was directed against the notion that causal relationships can be ascertained through *a priori* reasoning. He addressed particular attention to the connection between the present fact and that which is inferred from it, arguing that nothing so inferred can be guaranteed true in advance.

This is not our only problem, however. It is ontological knowledge and its many implications which confront us with a number of other problems, the nature of which bespeak a depth not encountered in other areas. As an example, Heidegger says without any hesitation that ontological knowledge turns out to be the problem of the essence of synthetic judgments *a priori*. This would mean that ontological knowledge, in the words of Heidegger, is judgment according to principles which must be brought forth without recourse to experience. Would this not require a "provisional characterization of that knowledge"? What does this say to our epistemological stance? The domain of the revelation of the origin of ontological knowledge is none other than that of the human mind.

While our total study in epistemology does not in any way emphasize the theories of Heidegger, at this point we permit him to raise additional questions which will be answered in other contexts. Does the essential unity of ontological knowledge always provide a basis for the determination of the essence of categories? Is it possible to speak of an ontological knowledge if it attains truth? Does ontological knowledge always form transcendence? If so, does formation hold open the horizon within which the Being of the essent is perceptible in advance? Does not ontological knowledge, the essential ground of which is supposedly the transcendental imagination, have, as essentially finite, an untruth corresponding to its truth? Is the only reason why ontological knowledge is made up of transcendental determinations of time because transcendence is temporalized in primordial time?

Putting all this together, is not our real question whether or not ontological knowledge proffers the setting in which the mind finds satisfactory answers to the questions addressed to it by the cognitive act?

Weigel and Madden raise an interesting point in discussing the phenomenologists, and the direction in Kant, whether or not he is true to the phenomenon of knowledge in supposing that the concept derives from the

Chapter Three: The Meaning of Knowledge

structural dynamism of knowledge. Is not the class notion content and not merely form? Windelband tells us we must start from the fundamental fact which underlies all logical reflection, namely, making a distinction, from the point of view of value, between the true and the false. Without question, he would have us believe that the phenomenology of knowledge is the "sum total of the empirical phenomena of knowledge which constitute the given presuppositions of logic as theoretical philosophy."

The question of the possibility of knowledge *a priori,* is not the problem. How can we *know* in advance that experience which should not conform to our principle will not be veridical, or will not be real in the category which is in question? asks Lewis. The former question can have no answer unless by some impossible dogmatism about the limitation of experience by a mind which is itself above or behind experience, and hence unknowable. And even this hypothesis of transcendent mind does not assure the permanence of its conditions unless by some further dogmatism which assume its continuity unchanged, Lewis adds.

Are the only preconditions of knowledge those suggested by Kant, namely, space and time? Did he not only consider these *a priori* preconditions of knowledge, but also for perception?

CHAPTER FOUR
FIVE DEFINITIONS

Ontology

Ontology is what epistemology is all about. Its concern is the *Being* of all existents. It is more than a science of analysis or inquiry; it is the art and science of determining the potentiality of all existence.

In the process of intellection, the mind works toward a comprehension of being; this is the learning process. In its movement toward comprehension, the mind brings to this process the objectified knowns which are possibly related to the object; to comprehend is to structure objectively the parts in relation to one another to form the whole of being. To relate parts, and parts to the whole is to determine the potentiality inherent in parts as well as in the whole. The mind is able to know being because it is transparent; it stands ready to reveal its essence when the mind is able to comprehend its form. Being is the totality of essence; it is what exists. The task of the mind is to objectify its essence; in this way, the mind learns why being exists. Essence and its meaning comprise being; the potential of what exists depends upon the mind and its powers of comprehension.

This power of comprehension is the prime transcendent factor in the intellective process. We must not forget that Kant raises his voice and demands to be heard the moment we introduce the "transcendent factor" into the argument. He raises the question: how are *a priori* synthetic judgments possible? While not in direct answer to his question, our response is this. Ontology is more than the science of philosophizing transcendentally. This is evident from our discussion above. But Heidegger discusses Kant's position by saying that when Kant wishes to characterize the problematic of traditional ontology, he makes use of the expression "transcendental philosophy" to denote the subject matter of metaphysical generalities (ontologia). This is why, in mentioning this traditional ontology, he speaks of the "transcendental philosophy of the ancients."

The problematic of which he speaks is the possibility of ontology being considered a problem.

We have mentioned the transparent factor in ontology. It is an important concern if we are to understand the implicative values inherent in ontology and its responsibility in the process of intellection. We must structure this force more thoroughly.

What makes an ontology possible? The transparency factor.

Essence possesses structure; to know essence is the ability to visualize the structural components of its being. Being comprises totality; to know essence is to determine the design of all constructs used in its formulation. In this way the "structure" of ontology becomes apparent by means of its visibility. No true learning takes place without this component in the intellective process.

Metaphysics

Metaphysics is the science of contemplation; it uses reason to transcend reason; it is the mind of the process of intellection; its task is to design the perspective of experience. Its basic contention is the belief that experience free knowledge is an impossibility.

All of this is another way of saying that the mind is not a receptor of knowledge. What is being suggested is this. As the mind functions, it recognizes its responsibility to the intuitive being which characterizes the ontological structure of its cognitive process. To meet this responsibility, the mind is constantly developing its powers of creativity, and it does this by means of the intuitive factors present in comprehension. It is correct to say, then, that metaphysics provides the implementation for the evolvement of value to be determined in the relationship between subject and object as this relationship develops synthetically from the experience of mind functioning through its empirical processes.

Truth resides not in representations, but in the ability of the mind to apprehend its relative values. Truth is absolute but its applicative values are relative. By degrees of apprehension, the mind must participate in the development of the criteria of truth and their-points of origination. It is these criteria which hold the greatest interest for the science of metaphysics.

The criteria of truth is first to be found in the material of knowledge, the object of the mind. Truth is; truth is being; what makes truth is its criterion.

Chapter Four: Five Definitions

To apprehend truth and its essence, the mind must function as directed by the leads inherent in the criteria. This is the internalization procedure which is an integral part of the process of intellection. Only through the operation of this process is it possible for the criteria of truth to be applied in the subject or mind. Descartes did not go far enough when he suggested changing the object into the subject's representation. Metaphysics is the science which makes it possible for the truth inherent in the object to be realized in its essence by the mind. It is the mind which universalizes the particulars of an object; metaphysics enables the mind to experience the material of knowledge and its meaning. This is a cognitive experience, as all experience is, analytically based on empirical methodology. To experience is to have found meaning; meaning is realized when relationships are validated through a verification of causal connections. Here is the thrust of an empirical methodology. It is metaphysics which provides the procedural lubricant, making it possible for the mind to function by means of its empirical perspective.

A fact is not a fact until those factors which make it a fact are determined. Until this happens, a fact is but a proposition, awaiting validation and verification. It is this transitional process which is dependent upon metaphysics for its direction. Direction suggests potentiality and potentiality suggests positivity, both of which are ingredients in the "becoming" process of interest to metaphysics. Potency is the ascendancy factor in potentiality; those factors which determine positivity, however, make it possible for the mind to move in the direction logically determined by validated method. Combine potentiality and positivity and you have the perspective of comprehension. To comprehend is to perceive what is "becoming" in the learning process, and what can become possible as being in action. Here is the science of metaphysics at work. It is a transcendental philosophy of methodology according to Kant's way of thinking. It concerns itself with totalities as universals; here is the whole question of ontology, what is possible for man to know and comprehend? Is there a difference between knowing and comprehension? If so, why, and in what ways?

These are questions which can be answered only by being conscious of the working premise of metaphysics. For the mind to function, it must rely on first principles, those which make it possible to comprehend the material of knowledge. Cause is oneness; it is the only means possible for the integration and unification of human knowledge. All being possesses cause; to determine its first principles is to discover its potentiality and the positivity of its presuppositions.

All thought evolves from presuppositions. However, while thought evolves from presuppositions, it is metaphysical thought which must analyze them and validate their *a priori* conditions. Metaphysics is that process of the mind which enables experience to transcend itself; that is, it qualifies experience for the process of experiencing its own conditions. These conditions are the primary qualities of reality; qualities alone make it possible for an object to be known. Thus, while they are *a priori,* it requires an empirical technique to discover their meaning. Qualities comprise the content of every object.

Reality is the matter of first principles; the qualities of the content of reality serve as the source of intention, realizable only by means of the inferential directives found in every concept; the concept is the working arm of the transcendental nature of the process of intellection.

The Foundations of Metaphysics

In one sense, metaphysics has a number of foundations upon which it builds its science of knowing. Strictly speaking, it has only one foundation, that is, *being.* It was suggested above that metaphysics forces the mind to concern itself with its own powers and potentialities. These questions loom large when the mind is confronted by its content. The moment the mind is concerned with potentiality, it is thinking in terms of ultimates. Thus, we have the chief of ontological problems, that of being. Metaphysics is based on the primary qualities of being. Metaphysics analyzes being as being. To make this analysis, the mind must examine the object in its relationship to the subject; that is, what potentialities are suggested by the object for consideration by the mind? This process is referred to by Kant; he alludes to it as the activity of our inner nature.

All experience comprises sensate reactions intellectually based on attributes of being. This is to say, the senses are empirical, to take a position opposite to that of Kant. Nothing can be imposed upon being; being imposes itself upon the self; being confronts itself. To do this, it intellectualizes its qualities as the embodiment of its content. This comprises the data of sensations.

Chapter Four: Five Definitions

Kant seems to think this is a difficult task. He says that it demands "a reader resolved to think himself gradually into a system which is grounded in nothing regarded as given except pure reason itself, and thus tries to develop knowledge out of its original seeds without seeking the support of any fact."

The problem here is that being is supported by fact; without fact, being cannot exist; without being, fact does not exist. Here is the crux of the ontological problem in epistemology. What takes place when we experience meaning is the comprehension of the material of knowledge. What takes place is a correlation of facts, in accordance with their nature, unifying existence and essence.

Metaphysics and the Traits of Existence

Metaphysics is the vehicle whereby existence experiences its own potential.

Qualities possess traits and metaphysics is primarily interested in the point of origination of each trait. Traits, which characterize content, make it possible for the mind to experience itself; in one sense, traits provide structure for existence, thereby language for the mind. It is the trait which equates content and essence; it possesses the potential for value. This is to remind the learner that all being is empirically rooted by means of its content and that value exists only as it evolves from that same being.

To think, there must be something to think about. These are ideas; ideas learn from ideas; this is the thought process. It is the mind at work on something. Because it is something, it has content and the mind analyzes content by its traits and their presuppositions. All of this is an intellectual experience; for the mind to experience, it must first experience itself and the truth which it possesses, even though it may still be in the form of assumptions. It is a movement toward certitude, basing its methodology upon presupposed knowns.

Truth is a trait of existence; it is truth which constantly purifies the process of intellection, as well as projecting the will as the determinant in the learning process.

The will supplies the mind with its power to think. This was of vital concern to Aristotle; it was a developmental thing for him; just how do we react to a confrontation? What use do we make of it? This is giving power to thought. His familiar words reminds us that "we should be grateful not only to those with whose views we may agree, but also to those who have expressed more superficial views; for those also contributed something, by developing, before us, the powers of thought."

Truth is metaphysical in nature; it is truth which provides the unity of all existence; it is truth which possesses the traits which reveal cause and its potentiality for becoming known. It is mind and its will which provides the process for the discovery of truth. Truth is the realization of intention couched in every existent.

The Mind of Metaphysics

Kant was most astute when he insisted that the thought process is dependent upon both metaphysical and empirical means. He failed to take into account, however, the fact that it is impossible to make a fine distinction between these means. When he says that the empirical factors are presented to the mind, and the metaphysical factors appear in the course of mental activity, the dichotomy between the two seemingly disappears when considered from the point of view of their interdependent factors. The paradoxical disease sets in when we recall that Kant "denied to metaphysics the character of science because for him experience was the product and the terminus of science, since science built it by applying to sensible data necessities which are pure forms of the mind."

One wonders if this same confusion was not experienced by Whitehead when, discussing the metaphysics of reality, he said that its scope embraces both perceiver and perceived. All is well up to this point. But then he goes on by saying that no perplexity concerning the object of knowledge can be solved by saying that there is a mind knowing it.

Nor, is this problem to be solved by making substitutions, as Comte would have us believe. His positivism required him to substitute science for metaphysics. The question he neglected to raise was this: how is content, the material of knowledge, to be received, if not by the mind? Being is received by being; here the mental and the material factors unite; this is the process of intellection.

Metaphysics, Science, and Experience

Metaphysics is concerned with existents, therefore, with what is real.

Chapter Four: Five Definitions

Reality is opened by the mind and investigated by the methodology structured by its metaphysical perspective. Metaphysics recognizes the existence of the absolute as cause of all being. Appearance serves as but a confrontation to the mind. Appearance bespeaks externals which must be subjected to the process of intellection to determine the nature of its reality. The mind must determine, therefore, ascertain the validity of the natural premises upon which appearance is based.

The highest and most sophisticated science of the natural order is metaphysics, according to St. Thomas. There is nothing more real than the natural order. The starting point of science is experience; to experience is to comprehend reality.

Without the metaphysical components of experience, science as methodology cannot function. This position can be documented when it is remembered that science functions methodologically through its assumptions pertaining to universals and particulars. Abstract universals require the experience inherent in intuition for their analysis; concrete universals require the experience inherent in intuition for their analysis. The difference, then? The same question can be raised about particulars.

Science raises this question about metaphysics. What is the object of metaphysics? Is it the universal? The particular? Or, is it, as we suggest, the point of origination as cause in both universals and particulars; the universal as transcendental is found in every particular. The object of metaphysics is the experienced substance of the trait of reality. Since experience is empirically based and functions according to its methodology, its material of knowledge serves as the assumptions of science.

Universals and particulars possess the potentiality for functional usage. It is the business of science to render these forces functional in the human mind. Existence is that which is universal and particular. It is an intelligible universe of mind identified together with content. Truth, as cause, is identical with existence, but only in its forms of potentiality, awaiting the process of experience by the mind. The mind, as being, examines its object, as being, in terms of the assumptions and potentiality of being. There is a logic in all of this; it is the logic of the scientific method. It demands a type of thinking based on reflective thought and structured according to the directives inherent in the science of perception. Its task is to formulate the criteria of reality. In

Chapter Four: Five Definitions

this way, metaphysics is not to be considered an end, but as means intimately related to method. Mind itself is means, the operant of cause. All truth, as cause, is dependent upon the science of metaphysics for its comprehension.

Rationalism

Rationalism has its epistemological foundation in experience; its goal is to determine the nature of reality; it toys with the *a priori* because there is the realization that in essence is found the true base of metaphysical existence.

Rationalism is a concept to be reckoned with in the theory of knowledge because it tells us that no learning takes place until the mind has learned to conceptualize its objects. This stance again raises the question of experience and its relationship to knowing. Is it possible to possess knowledge independent of experience? Kant says yes, and he points to mathematics as an example. Does this suggest that mathematics is the model of *a priori* knowledge? Is this what pure rationalism is telling us? How different is all this from Cartesian rationalism?

Both Kant and Descartes show concern for certainty in knowledge. As stated above, Kant pointed to mathematics as that subject which carries with it apodictic certainty. Here, he says, is an example of absolute necessity, not based on experience, and consequently a pure product of reason.

The question we ask is this. Is it possible to reason without experiencing the product of reason? Certainty is the realization of truth. To find meaning in truth is to know its essence, therefore, certain of its existence. As one reasons, one experiences. Does this mean Kant refuted rationalism? Or, was it the metaphysical base of experience which he refuted?

Popper discusses this problem, using Hegel to develop his argument. He asks: how did Hegel overcome Kant's refutation of rationalism? He answers: very easily, by holding that contradictions do not matter. They just have to occur in the development of thought and reason. They only show the insufficiency of a theory which does not take account of the fact that thought, that is reason, and with it (according to the philosophy of identity) reality, is not something fixed once and for all, but is developing. We live in a world of evolution, he says. Kant, says Hegel, refuted metaphysics, not rationalism. Popper continues. What Hegel calls metaphysics, he says, as opposed to dialectic, is only such a rationalistic system as does not take account of evolution, motion, development, and thus tries to conceive of reality as something stable, unmoved and free of contradictions. Hegel, with his philosophy of identity, infers that since reason develops, the world must develop, and since the development of thought or reason is a dialectic one, the world must also develop in dialectic triads.

There are innumerable problems raised for rationalism in the two preceding paragraphs, and which we have no intention of discussing here. But there is one problem which is impossible to by-pass: the essence of rationalism is the reasoning process. Again, we ask, is it possible to reason without experiencing its essence? To reason is to verify and confirm truth. Since experiencing is finding truth by means of its evidence, it includes what Kant and Hegel are insisting on, namely, not only is it necessary, in order to possess knowledge, to know what the object is, but how we must reason it as well.

The relevancy of a reasonable meaning is what true rationality is all about. Rationalism gives support to its reasons, for within its reasons resides its explanations. We must remember that it is the mind which reasons, and is able to do so because it has carefully structured the epistemological question, and which proffers explanations based on validated evidence.

Phenomenalism

There is one page in the history of phenomenalism which suggests a basic inconsistency. Lewis refers to it in this way: as the history of phenomenalism serves to illustrate, conceptual knowledge may be valid provided only there is order in experience — if experience is lawful — quite without reference to any further question.

The problem is not whether there is order in experience; this is the responsibility of the mind. When the mind experiences, it finds meaning; meaning is a resultant of the ordering experience. The problem lies in the referential quality of the relationship. For the mind to experience, it must experience something. Reference implies a relationship between things.

The relationship of which I speak is this. There is the tendency to suggest, by phenomenologists, that Humerian ideas and impressions are of such a nature that they take their stand between the knower and the thing or object to be known. Dewey raises his voice and tells us this position will have plenty of

Chapter Four: Five Definitions

support as long as sensations and ideas are supposed to be valid only when they report to mind something prior to them.

Ayer responds to this by saying that the phenomenalist need not deny that the manner in which sense-data occur can be explained in terms of entities which are not themselves observable; he will, however, add that to talk about such unobservable entities is, in the end, to talk about sense-data.

The question we must raise is whether or not the phenomenalist is not running head-on into a multitude of new problems when he holds that sense-data exists only when perceived, and that physical objects can exist without being perceived. Perhaps this is but another way of repeating the dicta of Ayer, without falling prey to the problem of entities.

Our problem here is with respect to the meaning of observation and perception. Köhler insists that in observation, quite apart from any theory, there is a dualism between percepts and their outer causes. And, he says, it is hard to interpret these and their outer causes. And it is hard to interpret these outer causes as though they again were merely percepts.

In keeping with this position, Ayer refers us to Plato's myth, the shadows on the wall of the cave, which are all that the prisoners can see, these are contrasted with substantial objects outside. Ayer raises the question: perhaps phenomenalism leaves us with nothing but the shadows.

But the mind isn't satisfied with shadows. What does the mind perceive, and why? Is the *what* of perception only an object? Is it possible to be means as well? Kant would have us believe that the real is not knowable in itself; the real does not inform thought; rather, thought informs the datum.

Are data, essences and ideas, as well as impressions, only means for knowing, not its objects? Here is a paradox. Dewey believes that as long as they are regarded as merely mental means rather than as means which through overt acts effect actual redisposition of antecedent things, the retort will have the character of an arbitrary *tour de force*, it will be a pious doctrine rather than a conclusion empirically verified.

We subject the above statement to the problem question raised: would data, or ideas, without being perceived, be true without benefit of observation? Does not perception intend to concern itself with the conditions of truth and the consciousness factor in experience? If so, where does this leave phenomenalism in the epistemological scheme of things?

Phenomenology

Phenomenology is that philosophy of experience which asks the questions, what is the essence of existence? And, what is the nature of the power used by the concept to justify its own process of analysis? These questions serve as the pivot of the mind's conscious activity in determining the potentiality of being for the purpose of uniting meaning and experience.

CHAPTER FIVE

THE EPISTEMOLOGICAL STANCE OF GIVENESS

Being

The Nature of Being

How does the epistemologist get at the problem of being when it is the totality of his being which is the subject doing the analysis? Aristotle says that it is not a simple process. As a matter of fact, he says, nothing is simple except the creator. He expressed this in his propositions concerning being. For him, being is composed of potency and act, substance and accidents. Potency, he does not want us to forget, is necessary to the distinction between the created and creator. The creator alone is simple.

Our problem then, is a complex one. The question, what is the nature of being? forces our being to define itself. Being is consciousness. Neither being nor consciousness can impose itself upon us because we *are* being and consciousness. Are they identical? If so, is it possible for them to possess different natures? A paradox? No.

Existence becomes a personal thing when I perceive its essence. If I should say that I perceive consciousness, it would be the same as saying that consciousness makes it possible for it to be conscious of itself. The same is true of being. The nature of being is found in its essence. It is understanding the nature of an existent which provides the mind with an explanation of the meaning of that existent.

It would not be imposing on our epistemological stance to say that being is what is real; but, this is not saying enough. Being is what is personally real. We do not hesitate to say there is reality independent of the mind and this reality has a being of its own, but it is an unactualized being, the essence of which is unknown. Steenberghen holds the position that being, the first affirmation, imposes itself as the absolute value of my knowledge and as the final end of my appetite for knowing. This is hardly the case. What is, as

Chapter Five: The Epistemological Stance of Giveness

being is, would find it paradoxical to place itself, as an imposition, upon itself. There is no question, being is the absolute realized value of all knowledge, but this is quite different from what Steenberghen is saying. Nor, would we agree with Descartes who keeps telling us to control being by knowledge. He seems to forget that knowledge becomes the essence of being, indeed, the mind of being.

There are eight premises upon which we build our definition of the nature of being.

First, Being is caused. This position presents us with no particular problem in so far as definitive meanings are concerned. Regis helps us to understand cause in relation to being when he says that the philosophical meanings of cause can be reduced to four, two of which express the thing in its intrinsic constitutive elements, matter and form, while the other two express the orientation of being and its different activities, the efficient and final causes.

We move to the heart of our consideration when this question is asked, is there a condition upon which the existence of cause depends? The answer is no. However, the answer is yes when we ask, is there a condition upon which the existence of what is caused depends? There is but one existent which may be termed an entity; this is cause. All other existents evolve from it, therefore, are caused. The conditions for existence are those which bring what can be caused into being. The essence of being stems from the substance of what is potential in cause.

Second. Existence is the actualization of the essence of being. Another way of positing this proposition is to use the words of Maritain. There is, he says, a vigorous correspondence between knowledge and immateriality. A being is a knowing being to the extent that it is immaterial. We must not let his use of a being distract us. Hawkins tells us the reason. Ontological analysis reveals, he insists, a distinction of being and individual quiddity within the unity of things.

This is the reason Maritain speaks of the ontological explanation, and which we insist on using to define our proposition. At this point in our analysis, Maritain places a severe limit upon the ontological by confining it to the first degree of abstraction, that is, in the order of sensible and observable

Chapter Five: The Epistemological Stance of Giveness

data. He explains this by saying the mind enters that order in the search for their intimate nature and intelligible reasons. That is, why, in following this path, it arrives at notions like corporeal substance, quality, operative potency, material or formal cause, etc., notions which, while they bear reference to the observable world, do not designate objects which are themselves representable to the senses and expressible in the image — or a spatio-temporal scheme. Such objects, he continues, are not defined by observations or measurements to be effected in a given way.

While we agree with Maritain in his basic assumptions and presuppositions, in a sense, these by-pass the thrust of our problem. It all centers on the giveness of being. We question whether being is something given to the mind, especially when we hold that mind is the embodiment of being, and the totality of being is mind. There is an inconsistency here in the projection of Maritain when, on the one hand, he says that being is the first thing given to the mind, but, on the other hand, it is impossible, he believes, to think of a pure object separated from an ontological "stuff" possessing existence for itself or capable of so possessing it. He unravels this paradox by positing the proposition: it is impossible to think a pure object separated from a being for itself, a being of which the object of sensation or understanding is but a determination or aspect. This, of course, could not happen if we move on the premise that the totality of being is mind. To this, he would reply in question, if such an object is not an aspect of a known thing, of a trans-objective thing, will it then not become an aspect of the knowing thing?

To which, we answer: among the limitations of mind is one which refers to its own limitations, namely, the mind is unable, as being, to conceive anything which might transcend being. This means that since mind functions by means of its ideas, the being of an idea then becomes the absolute for the mind. Being exists as the totality of the potential in every existent. This is the "stuff" of ontology.

Third. While the intellect is the embodiment of being, the intellect becomes the object of being. Here, again, we may be tempted to say this is a paradox.

It is not a paradox, and these are the reasons. They are three in number. The mind learns only as it conceptualizes its object. Now, while the mind is being, the object is likewise being; the process of conceptualization fuses the

Chapter Five: The Epistemological Stance of Giveness

being of subject and object into what comes to be known; being is then the embodiment of the intellective process and the intellective process is the embodiment of being. Only in this way does the mind understand itself as being. It is mind which experiences the intentionality of cause as evidenced by its effects. Here is the clearest indication of the meaning of cause, namely, its means of expression, effect. Being is greater than the becoming object because of its inherent potentialities.

Fourth. Being is always an existent. This is true even if it is the being resident in the intentionality and potentiality of cause. Being is the idea of potency, therefore, an existent in mind as well as in cause.

Five. It is possible to say, then, because of the potency dimension, being is act. This, of course, is the position of St. Thomas. It is a warranted stand. "Only by reference to being do the complex components of the real deserve the title of act."

What does all of this mean? It alerts us to the fact of movement by being and in being. Moreover, by means of being, the real is actualized because of its qualities. Essence is known because of its attributes; the quality of attributes holds the potential for the mind's actualization of existence. It is an attribute which makes it possible for the mind to define an object. Definitions evolve from the premises from which the attributes are deduced.

Six. It is being as act and potentiality which provides the mind with the opportunity to conceive being as being. It is being which defines itself; this it does according to its attributes. Thus, it becomes a problem in epistemology.

To define itself it must know itself. Here is act with the potentiality of self realization. To understand being is to know the qualities of its attributes.

Seven. To conceive being as being is to be aware of being. Here is a problem which confronted Hawkins. Awareness, he says, is primarily an awareness of being. "What we are primarily aware of is, then, a succession of states of being."

Eight. To be aware of being is the ontological base from which the cognitive act evolves. This is why we say all being is a process of becoming. It is, but is in the process of moving beyond its cause. Hawkins calls this the metaphysic of becoming in terms of being.

Chapter Five: The Epistemological Stance of Givenness

The way we wish to characterize being at this junction in our discussion is to say, by the potentiality of its power. It is the quality of its attributes which prepare the setting in which the power inherent in being is realized.

The most powerful attribute of being is truth. When fact conforms to truth, being is actualized and realized as the totality of itself. At this point knowledge is recognized as being. Being, because of its nature, seeks only for self-fulfillment, the same goal determined by the intellective process.

The Affirmation of Being

How do we determine the absolute value of knowledge? By means of the affirmative of being.

Steenberghen explains my question and answer. He tells us that the affirmation of being realizes the ideal of perfect knowledge, the absolute value or goal of knowledge. Why? Because this affirmation possesses a truth which is absolutely evident and certain. However, this ideal is realized in consciousness in a very imperfect way. It follows that, while it gives me a norm which will allow me to evaluate the other elements of my knowledge, the affirmation of being leaves my appetite for knowing only partially satisfied.

The Concept of Being

This consciousness of which he speaks. What does it portend for the unification found in every true conceptualization process? Really, only one thing. The concept of being encompasses all of the dimensions of reality. Here is the power of the concept. It lies within the functional ability of the mind in the process of conceptualization to delineate the simple within the complex and relate parts to a whole.

The Experience of Being

It is being which enables the mind (while itself is being) to experience reality. Experience is the only means by which the mind is confronted by the potential of the real from within the values of existence. It is at this point in the intellective process the mind realizes itself as being.

Finite Being

Finite being is characterized by the limitations of his power for reason. But, because he does have the power, as Heidegger reminds us, to make the horizon intuitive, that is, of forming spontaneously the aspect of that which is capable of offering itself, to do this, he has the power to think. Intuition is based on this power to think; the finitude characterizes his intuitive perspective rather than the operational cause assumed in the cognitive act.

The Idea of Being

What is the essence of consciousness? In one sense, this is asking, what constitutes content of consciousness? The answer is *idea.* What ideas, then, do I possess about being? Especially, when I know that ideas evolve from being? Moreover, because they are being? Ideas are real; is it possible for what is real to reflect the real? Or, is it because ideas are real they possess the ability to reflect the real? We respect the latter position.

If the idea is a matter of content, it must be considered as the data of consciousness. As data, it possesses value and must be recognized as such; herein lies the function of the mind as it becomes conscious of the relationship between an idea and its referent.

Knowledge of Being

Nothing is given the mind when the mind experiences meaning. Giveness is resident in experience. While it is our position that existents exist outside of experience (and must so exist in order for us to have something to experience) meaning is realized only when an existent is experienced; that is, brought within the being of mind. When meaning has been achieved, knowledge has been gained, and being has been actualized. In this way, mind possesses knowledge of the real, which I consider as experiencing the potentiality of being. Here is the only way the mind is able to actualize being and its attributes.

Chapter Five: The Epistemological Stance of Giveness

Cause

A Definition

Ducasse states the obvious when he tells us that philosophers have been loose, vague and inconsistent in their statements concerning causation. Perhaps Russell is a prime example. Perhaps not. To provide us with some idea of the difficulties we face in definition, Weigel reminds us that Mill, like Bacon, explained things by what they called "cause," which is not at all what Aristotle or Thomas meant. In Mill it means only the active determining principle in the thing, and for him the principle of determinism and the principle of causality are identical. Thus, the determining principle which explains the phenomenon is given by sheer observation, and observation induced the induction spontaneously. Cause can then be defined as "the sum total of conditions, positive and negative taken together."

What are our problem areas, then? We list four. One. Does cause mean something different from "invariable antecedent?" Russell raises this question. Two. Is cause necessary for every event? Hume says no because it is possible to conceive of some event now occurring without also conceiving of a cause for that event. Three. Is cause only an antecedent? Or, is cause the antecedent which, if manipulated, regulates the occurrence of the consequent? Dewey seems to think so. Four. Ducasse, in a discussion on Mill, suggests cause should be contrasted with condition. The cause of a phenomenon, he says, is a change in its antecedent circumstances which was sufficient to bring it about. A condition of a phenomenon on the other hand, is a change, or more frequently a state, of its antecedent circumstances which was necessary to its having occurred when it did.

What has been said above is enough to suggest that it is almost impossible to define cause without noting its relationships through effect.

Chapter Five: The Epistemological Stance of Givenness

The Cause-Effect Relationship

We are reluctant to accept Hume's position on the cause-effect relationship at face value. You will recall he says the relationship exists when two objects are constantly conjoined: *a* is the cause of *b* is the occurrence of *a* is invariably followed by the occurrence of *b*. This is the reason we listed the first problem area as perhaps being the most suggestive. This relationship raises many questions in our mind. For instance: just because we distinguish cause from effect, does this imply that cause is earlier than effect? Russell is the one who asks us to use the word earlier. Is cause a postulate of the mind? If so, what provides the *a priori* with content and potentiality? Does Dewey answer these questions when he insists that for knowledge cause and effect alike have a partial and truncated being? His use of the word truncated has the tendency to add to the confusion. He is clearer in his exposition when he tells us that a relationship of cause-effect has been transformed into one of means-consequence. Consequences, he says, belong to the conditions which may produce them, and the latter possess character and distinction. The meaning of causal conditions is carried over also into the consequence, so that the latter is no longer a mere end, a last and closing term of arrest. It is marked out in perception, distinguished by the efficacy of the conditions which have entered into it. Its value as fulfilling and consummatory is measurable by subsequent fulfillments and frustrations to which it is contributory in virtue of the causal means which compose it.

Hume refers to objects as causes and effects. To hold this position, he insists that all reasonings concerning cause and effect are founded on experience, and that all reasonings from experience are founded on the supposition that the course of nature will continue uniformly the same. Like causes, in like circumstances, will always produce like effects.

To this stand, Ducasse raises some objection. If by an object is meant, he says, a thing such as a tree, or a stone, or a piece of lead, or a

Chapter Five: The Epistemological Stance of Giveness

mountain, or a man, and the like-as in fact mostly is the case — we cannot then properly speak of an object as being a cause or an effect. We indeed say, loosely, that the mountains cause the early dusk of the valley; but we willingly acknowledge that what we really mean is that the position of the mountains with regard to the valley, and to the sun's course, causes the earliness of dusk in the valley.

We still have not located the core of our problem. Perhaps we will find it in our discussion of cognitive cause.

Cognitive Cause

Perhaps this is a dimension of cause seldom analyzed because of the kinds of questions it raises. The moment we are ready to handle the problems of cognitive cause, we are confronted with the *nature* of the object of knowledge. Such a confrontation should stop the epistemologist in his intellective tracks until he is aware of his need for, and dependency upon, philosophical analysis, as suggested by Guzie. This is accomplished, says Guzie, in an examination of the cognitive aspects of learning. There is a need here to trace the cognitive causes of lower forms of learning. This analysis will be used primarily to bring into focus the nature of that type of learning directly entailing disciplined intellectual knowledge.

The Necessity of Cause

Since there is the need to trace cognitive causes, we take a stand opposite to that held by Hume who says that we can never demonstrate the necessity of a cause to every new existence, or new modification of existence, without showing at the same time the impossibility there is that anything can ever begin to exist without some productive principle; and where the latter proposition cannot be proved, he says, we must despair of ever being able to prove the former.

Seemingly, there is some inconsistency between the foregoing, and what he now has to say. An attempt is made to right himself by saying that since it is not from knowledge or any scientific reasoning that we

Chapter Five: The Epistemological Stance of Giveness

derive the opinion of the necessity of a cause to every new production, that opinion must necessarily arise from observation and experience.

We ask at this point, if Hume believed that knowledge *is* experience, what changes would he have to make in his position?

He side-steps the real question by asking another. How does experience give rise to such a principle? He answers it by saying: But as I find it will be more convenient to sink this question into the following, why we conclude that such particular causes must necessarily have such particular effects, and why we form an inference from one to another? We shall make that the subject of our future inquiry 'twill, perhaps, be found in the end that the same answer will serve for both questions.

The Idea of Cause

Such consideration forces us to ask, what is the idea of cause? From where does the idea come? Is it possible to equate the idea with the beginning of an existent? Does not an existent evolve from cause? Does this make the idea and cause identical? Perhaps it is necessary, in order to demonstrate the necessity of cause, to separate the idea of cause from the beginning of an existent. Or, would this further confuse us by suggesting there is a plurality of cause?

The Plurality of Causes

Or, is there the suggestion that there is needed a plurality of ideas in order to arrive at the idea of cause? Russell favors the plurality of causes approach. Watkin interprets this to mean a plurality of causes explaining the same event, a distinct series of antecedent events mutually closed issuing in the same final consequent. But we should let Russell speak for himself: It may well be that the same system which is susceptible of material determinants is also susceptible of mental determinants; thus a mechanical system may be determined by sets of volitions as well as by sets of material facts.

Chapter Five: The Epistemological Stance of Giveness

Efficient Cause

Dewey was adamant in his belief that the aim of science is to determine extrinsic relations instead of intrinsic forms, as well as the search for efficient causes instead of for final causes.

What is efficient cause? It is what is uncaused. To say it another way: it *is* what is uncaused.

Watkin explains our position. The argument, he says, from motion or change to a First Mover or source of change is a special application of the argument from sufficient reason and causality. Both arguments, the narrower argument from change and the wider argument from sufficient reason under which the former is subsumed, are reducible to a discrimination of the formal category of causedness intellected (intuited) in contingent being. For causedness is the dependence of being which has come into existence upon a sufficient ground of its coming into existence. But this dependence upon a sufficient ground is a contingence upon it. Therefore the discrimination of causedness is a particular discrimination of the wider formal category of contingence which when held in the focus of contemplation is seen to involve an Absolute Ground. Nor can this Absolute Ground be the universe as a whole, the sum total of particular effects. For a sum of beings, all of which are caused, cannot be uncaused.

The efficient cause is the absolute. Only an absolute is uncaused, only the absolute is the single power "which causes knowledge and makes us conscious of truth."

Final Cause

What is this Absolute Ground? St. Thomas calls Him God. We agree. But for purposes of continuity of argument, we are taking the liberty to substitute absolute for God in the stand of St. Thomas. His definition of Final Cause is one we cannot afford to ignore. We paraphrase the statement of Regis: The final cause is a kind of sharing in the infinite perfection of the absolute by adding to our own being all the excellences that we find in beings outside of ourselves. Everything that is, is the realization of the idea of cause and possesses an ontological truth. And formal truth consists in the immanent enjoyment of all these ideas which the absolute has projected into the world, and thus in a gradual building up of our being which makes us draw closer and closer to our model of the absolute. Using these truths as the rungs on the ladder of being, we shall ascend slowly toward the truth whose possession will be our eternal happiness. And it is here that wisdom intervenes to make a hierarchy of all the truths that man possesses, to distinguish between the fallible and infallible sources of truth, to judge of the richness of the evidence and certitude of each truth, to join the proper object of human intelligence, which is material being, to its final object which is the absolute.

Formal Cause

We are aware, of course, that Aristotle ranked the formal cause above the material cause. But are we aware of his reasons for making this distinction? Cassirer assists us here by saying that purpose is the true and original essence and universal moving principle. Whoever wants to study nature, he says, must go back to the supreme cause. The operations of this cause can no longer be described in purely mechanical terms. This God moves the world without being in material contact with it and without himself being moved by it. He acts merely through his own being, by his all-embracing presence, and not by force and impact.

If Aristotle would agree with this interpretation is open to question. However, we need not be in question as to the stand St. Thomas takes on this matter. As we quote Regis now, the reader is asked to do his own paraphrasing. The formal cause is being, St. Thomas says, the total object of our knowledge. All that we know as true, whether it be sensible or intelligible, we know as being. For the object of a power and of its activity, is precisely the form of the object. This form is analogical, it embraces realities utterly diverse, such as first matter and

Chapter Five: The Epistemological Stance of Giveness

God, as it mounts on the ladder of being whose rungs are the ascendant gradients of reality. All this is the very life of intelligence as it apprehends things under the aspect of being. There, indeed, is the mystery of knowledge which rationalism cannot explain and of which only the intuition that characterizes every intelligence can give a satisfactory account.

Material Cause

The difficulty in defining material cause lies in our definitive attitude toward the absolute. If we say the Absolute Ground, as cause, is immaterial, and stands to be apprehended by what is material, our problem vanishes. If we say the Absolute Ground, as cause, possesses the essence of which is material, our problems have only started.

A second area of concern lies with the essence of intelligence. Is it material or immaterial? Does cause evolve from intelligence? Is this what we mean by material cause? If cause evolves from intelligence, cause is no longer cause. Or, if we say that material cause is intelligence, what exists as premises upon which intelligence reacts? We question why Regis suggests that material cause is intelligence, the only possible subject of true knowledge. He defends this statement by saying that truth, with its demands of duality and synthesis, can be found only in the judgment of the intellectual power. He further believes that intelligence is the sole reservoir of all our truths, whatever be their nature.

If we are willing to say that intelligence has first been caused, and now becomes cause because of its responsibility as an integral part of the cognitive process, we are closer to an understanding of material cause. Intelligence makes it possible for the material of cause to be actualized; intelligence makes it possible for the mind to experience the material of knowledge.

Extrinsic Cause

While we have disagreed in part with Regis with respect to material cause, his definitions of extrinsic and intrinsic cause give us a profound insight into these epistemological components.

Extrinsic cause link substances to each other in a hierarchy of perfection according to nature and existing; ultimately they blend into an absolute unity, when absolute efficiency, exemplarity, and finality meet in Him who is Being.

Intrinsic Cause

Intrinsic causes are none other than that which defines reality as composite, whether this composition is that of a nature from matter and form or that of a being from essence and esse. It is the principle of identity, in the philosophical sense of this word, that simultaneously governs the distinction between compositive elements and their unity as natural and as being.

The Meaning of Cause

We are now ready to define cause. We structure our definition upon the following propositions.

1. Cause is the embodiment of being which is uncaused. This means the totality of cause is its being, unlimited in potentiality.

2. Cause is without beginning. However, beginning evolves from the conditions which make it possible for cause to declare its intention, and for intelligence to apprehend the potentiality inherent in the intention.

3. Cause is the reason for the nature of the effect.

4. Since cause is its being, becoming evolves from the inherent potentiality of cause.

5. Resident in cause is the reason and explanation for change.

6. Cause can be understood only in its being as related to what *is*.

7. In point of reference, therefore time, cause exists in order to bring effect into being. Only in this way is cause able to maintain

Chapter Five: The Epistemological Stance of Givenness

"uniformity of sequence."

8. To experience cause the mind must find meaning in first principles.

9. Cause is the productive principle underlying the process of becoming as being strives to actualize itself by means of its potentialities.

10. It is cause alone which determines when effect *is*.

11. It is the human mind which experiences the intention of cause, therefore, revealing its purpose. What is known to us of cause evolves not only from a knowledge of effects, but from the metaphysical premises inherent in the teleological principles resident in cause.

12. Cause is the sum of all premises of being.

What is cause, then?

Cause, as the productive principle of being, reveals its intentionality by means of its effects; effects are the actualities of the potential of cause. Cause possesses no antecedents and thus, no conditions for its existence; whatever change cause precipitates in effect is resident in its being. Cause, as absolute, exists as the meaning of meaning, awaiting to be experienced by the human mind. From cause, what *is,* evolves.

Causality

What is the operational difference between cause and causality? Perhaps the prime distinction would be to suggest that causality is a category. Cassirer calls it a general category that extends over the whole field of human knowledge, one not restricted to a particular realm, to the world of material phenomena. Perhaps a clearer distinction is seen when cause is considered the source of law; when this is posited, we see what Popper means when he says causality means determination by law.

Kant is correct when he insists that causality is the presupposition which makes science possible. We can now say that causality is the

Chapter Five: The Epistemological Stance of Giveness

functional category which enables cause to become operant. Both Popper and Weigel discuss quite freely the deterministic dimension of causality. For instance: the law of causality, which means the law of universal determinism of the present by the past along an irreformable pattern, was and is an instrument of scientific procedure. Our point of hesitancy revolves about their definition of determinism. If they mean, like Köhler, that causality implies determination and prediction, we are clear in our thinking, especially if we can equate prediction and intentionality.

The use of intentionality is more to our liking because it suggests there is a principle of causality rather than the baldness of a law of causality. Without question, there is a law of causality, but, what are the principles which underlie its formulation and determination? Whenever we deal in principles, there is the implication that the touch of the ontological has been felt. The ontological is given priority when causality is looked upon as principles. Also, it completely changes the nature of the deterministic thrust. Hawkins underlines each of the foregoing words when he says we can conceive of something as being caused without having begun to exist but existing in an eternal causal dependence. This, of course, can mean only one thing. Because causality is principle, what is caused is determined as being, something considered *a priori,* therefore different from what is brought into being. What is caused is what it is because of the principles of causality underlying the being of cause.

It is only experience that can decide what cause is; it is only the principles of causality which can determine the nature of the is. It is for this reason we suggest that causality is a category; the category of causality is based on experience.

Meaning

There is but one non-existent, knowledge without meaning. For this reason, meaning is generic. Meaning resides in the material of knowledge; it is ready to share its implications with the human mind.

Chapter Five: The Epistemological Stance of Givenness

Meaning then, is the resultant of the intellectual action of the mind; it is the result of a method of learning applied to an object.

Meaning cannot be identified as the object of learning. The originality of meaning evolves from what the object or knowledge *is* and portends. When the mind finds meaning, it means that the implicative qualities of knowledge and its object have been translated into a language understandable by the mind.

The Meaning of Meaning

Experience does not possess meanings; it experiences them. As experience experiences meaning, it identifies the relational impressions which an object reveals and leaves on the mind. Meaningfulness exists when the relational qualities depicting the intention of an object through its purpose is experienced.

Meanings are propositions because of their value as an actualized existent, but even more so because of their potentiality as an experiential value. Meaning generates value; herein lies its intention. The purpose of meaning is to discover yet greater depths in its own being.

The concept meaning, like the concept knowledge, is dependent upon the thought visualization process which is translatable into words for its impact in the mind. As Polanyi tells us, words are the carriers of meaning.

Meaning is understood in terms of judgment. True judgment implies that the process of conceptualization is functioning. Meaning is predicated knowledge; to determine meaning is to bring its referential values into being. This is the procedure used by the mind to give meaning to words. Words are the actualization process which identifies meaning in ideas. Words are the instruments used to assure effectiveness in judgment. It is this concept of judgment, in relation to meaning, which insists there can be no distinctions made in the structure of meaning; when meaning is found, it implies there has been breadth and depth of thought given to its object. Both breadth and depth of thought in meaning are dependent upon the potentiality of what is to be known. The material of knowledge and its meaning becomes actualized only because of the potentiality of its knowability. Actual knowledge makes theoretical knowledge realizable. This is the reason we say that meaning is both universal and transcendent.

The Task of the Mind in Meaning

What has been said above forces us to answer this question, what is the task of the mind in meaning? The answer is this. To react to what it has brought into being as meaning, and then use it in order to learn even more. The problem is this: it's no problem for the mind to react, but it becomes a problem for the mind to use meaning.

By nature, the mind functions best in accordance with ideals which it has generated. Ideals are transcendent factors; to find meaning is to transcend the object by understanding its nature, scope and purpose. Every object, as the material of knowledge, possesses ideals. These culminate in what they want to become in the human mind. Ideals are communicated by the object through their actualization in meaning by the mind.

Every transcendent methodology particularizes its universals. Only in this way is it able to objectify meaning. Meaning is the dynamic force which makes it possible for consciousness to plumb its own depths; herein lies the chosen means for ascertaining potentiality in existence. The mind uses meaning to find meaning.

Cognitive Meaning

All meaning is factual; this is the reason we said that every transcendent methodology particularizes its universals in order to objectify meaning. It is objectified meaning which has intellectual significance. Actual meaning is strengthened by the potentiality of what an objectively structured fact implies. What possesses intellectual significance, then, is instrumental. This is what Lewis had in mind,

Chapter Five: The Epistemological Stance of Giveness

when discussing the meaning of meaning, said: our reference to past events is a special kind of reference to future ones. Within this movement, it is the cognitive process which brings meaning to its point of becoming meaningful.

Belief

Is it possible for belief to transcend experience? Here is our epistemological problem.

Elements in Belief: Working Hypotheses

The source of belief is time.

Belief is a stance of the mind, a reaction to what has been experienced as real. In this sense, belief is memory. Thus, all belief has an external referent.

Belief is the resultant of the operant relationship between cause and effect. Perception of change is the given in this characteristic of belief.

Reasons for belief arise from cause. Propositions, then, are inherent in belief, and become identical with belief when adopted.

The function of belief resides in its powers of motivation. Herein lies the momentum for the transition of thought.

Belief is the sense of identification, a belonging to an object.

Belief is open always to new dimensions of belief.

Belief is expressed in the thought of words.

Belief is caused by belief.

Belief in conclusions evidences belief in their premises.

All beliefs are inferred in their origins.

The analysis of belief is predicated on the analysis of causation.

The Expression of Belief

Reasons for belief are inherent in the belief; to express belief is to

Chapter Five: The Epistemological Stance of Giveness

voice attitudes in support of the reasons which comprise the being of belief. The expression of belief is a statement of judgment of what *is*.

Belief: An Expression of Words

Perhaps the main characteristic of belief is the fact that it is always expressed by means of the thought expressed in words. Belief cannot exist unless it is a mode of communication, if only with the self. In belief, the mind knows what it possesses. Language is the expression of the thought of belief.

Belief and Acquaintance

Acquaintance does not presuppose experienced meaning; therefore, there is no belief which is identical with acquaintance. Belief is always belief that. (Woozley)

Belief and Judgment

Belief is the act of judgment, a "complex unity brought out by the operation of judging, which is true if corresponding to it there is another complex unity consisting of the objects of the judgment arranged in the order in which they are arranged in the judgment complex." (Woozley)

Belief and Ideas

Ideas evolve from ideas; ideas learn from ideas. Belief evolves from ideas; belief is strengthened by ideas.

Feeling cannot be equated with belief; the implicative values are not strong enough, unless they have been objectified. A feeling for an idea does not validate the idea, nor even subject it to the mind as the embodiment of experience. Belief is not something felt by the mind; rather, it is the mind experiencing, therefore, believing, (in) its object. Belief is actualized by the mind when the mind experiences meaning as idea.

Chapter Five: The Epistemological Stance of Giveness

Belief and Attitude

Belief is a reflection of attitude, a statement of principle advocating the fulfillment of the intention of cause.

Belief and Certainty

To know is to experience meaning; within meaning lies certainty. Belief is to know the material of knowledge; here is certainty.

The Validity of Belief

Dewey looks upon belief as a tool; belief is warranted if it is a cause of satisfaction. He places this tenet along side his thinking about consequences. Consequences he says, can be accepted as tests of validity provided these consequences are operationally instituted and are such as to resolve the specific problem evoking the operation. Russell would agree in part but adds that when an empirical belief is true, it is true in virtue of a certain occurrence which he calls its verifier.

The validity of belief operates within the construct of value. It is value and its realization which portends the degree of meaningfulness in belief and the determination of its validity. What consequences evolve from belief because the value of the object has been realized? Here is the crux of the validity problem for belief.

The Evidence of Belief

While Woozley raises more questions than are answered, he posits a number of problems with respect to evidence and belief. He tells us belief covers six cases: (1) Being sure and being right, on evidence which is not conclusive; (2) Being sure and being wrong, on evidence which is not conclusive; (3) Being unsure and being right, on evidence which is not conclusive; (4) Being unsure and being wrong, on evidence which is not conclusive; (5) Being unsure and being right, on evidence which is conclusive; (6) Being sure and being right, on evidence which is conclusive.

Chapter Five: The Epistemological Stance of Giveness

It is case six which, he says, is not a case of believing, but of knowing.

What are the implications of evidence on belief? Since questions themselves carry value directives, questions will be raised to answer our question.

What is the value of evidence? Is there an intentionality in value and its relationship to evidence? Is the nature of evidence one of rationality? Is evidence ever to be considered as an entity? Does belief in existence depend wholly upon evidence? Does existence depend upon evidence for its existence? Is there a fallibility to belief because of the fallibility of evidence? Are there degrees of adequacy of belief, or degrees of adequacy of evidence?

The Degrees of Belief

"There are admittedly various degrees of belief and our beliefs are changing. But a belief does not cease to exist merely because it is weak or because it is variable" (Polanyi).

Class of Beliefs

It is Russell who speaks of *class of beliefs.*

We assume in practice that a class of beliefs may be regarded as true if (a) they are firmly believed by all who have carefully considered them, (b) there is no positive argument against them, (c) there is no known reason for supposing that mankind would believe them if they were untrue.

The most obvious class of beliefs not caused by other beliefs are those that result directly from perception. These, however, are not the only beliefs that are psychological premises. Others are required to produce our faith in deductive arguments. Perhaps induction also is based, psychologically, upon primitive beliefs. (Russell)

Chapter Five: The Epistemological Stance of Giveness

Belief and Value

Whether belief is caused by other beliefs, or by perception is not our problem here. Whenever we speak of class we admit categories. Categories force us to take cognizance of value. Value cannot be separated from belief; it is value which brings belief into being and gives it meaning. Since value is predicated on qualities and belief is the actualization of the assertative characteristic of qualities, the relationship between value and belief is tempered by the realization of intention evidenced by the valuations proffered by every premise. Cause in the source of quality; within qualities alone lie meaning.

Belief and Experience

The relationship between belief and experience is one of Russell's favorite topics. For instance, he would like us to believe that beliefs which transcend the experience of the believer always involve variables in their expression. To this he adds: but some beliefs whose expression involves variables do not transcend experience, and among these some are basic. He then proceeds to make things more difficult for himself by saying that some beliefs must express personal experience, the only extension being that the experience may be recollected. "The experience concerned must be mine and no one else's. Everything that I learn from others involves variables..."

There are a number of points here that are apt to lead us astray.

Is it possible for an act of mind (belief) to transcend experience when that act itself functions as experience? It is true that beliefs express personal experience, but not as a process of recollection. Experience fuses itself to experience in the same way an idea learns from an idea, thus bringing an idea into being. Experience makes it possible for experience to exist as being. The mind experiences; it does not have an experience.

To believe is to believe something; it is the mind experiencing its object and finding meaning. What is believed is experience. Belief comes together with experience. Experience makes meaning intelligible.

Belief and Fact

We stated that to believe is to believe something. Does this imply that what we believe is a fact? If it does, it puts us in the position of being the determinant of what constitutes fact. What makes a fact fact? When is a fact fact?

When belief exists, there is a fact which is this something of which we spoke above? Is the impact of the relationship between belief and fact one of intent only? How does one know when his belief is true? If we know our belief is true, does this intellectual stance set aside belief in favor of knowledge? Does this not suggest that belief is knowledge, and knowledge implies belief. Does the mind distinguish belief from knowledge? Is it enough to suggest that what makes a true belief is fact?

Belief and Knowledge

Woozley attacks our problem by saying that

knowledge and true belief might be different even though their objects were the same, because the relation of knowing was different from the relation of believing; and, secondly, it might be possible to be aware of a fact and yet not to recognize that it was a fact, just as one can meet an American and yet fail to recognize him as an American.

Woozley is open to the suggestion that the increase in "rational belief may become (and often does become) knowledge, namely, when the evidence increases to the point of becoming conclusive."

To this, Russell would ask, you acquire a true belief as to the time of day, but would it be correct to say that you have a knowledge of the time? Is what Russell is saying to imply that it is impossible to believe and to know at the same time?

Chapter Five: The Epistemological Stance of Giveness

Perhaps the crux of our problem is to ask: is the justification of belief found only in cause? If so, what are the implications for any theory of knowledge? Certainly this would not imply that belief is the means of revealing knowledge? Certainly this would not imply that belief is mere acceptance of what we wish to know.

Nor, would we hesitate to ask: is belief the source of all knowledge? As Polanyi would have us believe:

> We must now recognize belief once more as the source of all knowledge. Tacit assent and intellectual passions, the sharing of an idiom and of a cultural heritage, affiliation to a like-minded community: such are the impulses which shape our vision of the nature of things on which we rely for our mastery of things. No intelligence, however critical or original, can operate outside such a fiduciary framework.

Polanyi may be suggesting that belief is a matter of method; it may even suggest that data are more certain than the belief which evolves from them. If all of this is true, we must ask, is belief prepositional rather than knowledge? If belief is a matter of method, does this eliminate knowing as procedural in nature, as well as propositional?

Or, perhaps one should approach our problem in this way. If we make a distinction between belief and knowledge, on what cognitive basis is each to be defined? Is belief a matter of pure subjectivity? And knowledge, a matter of pure objectivity?

What about the element of control? Does belief control knowledge? Does knowledge control belief? Is it realistic to suggest that control is necessary? Dewey tells us that knowledge is the method of criticizing belief; it is the method of determining right participation in beliefs on the part of personal factors.

What are these personal factors? They are relevant only when a distinction is made between belief and knowledge. This distinction is predicated on the position that knowledge cannot be false, but belief

Chapter Five: The Epistemological Stance of Giveness

can be false. Does this mean there are contingent truths?

Belief and Truth

Perhaps the first conclusion which might be drawn from what has been said is this: there is a relation between belief and fact. Woozley calls this a relation of correspondence. He adds: there is a relation of non-correspondence between a false belief and the facts. False belief cannot have facts for its accusatives, and must therefore have something else.

What, then, is a true belief? When is a belief true? For our second conclusion, we wish to state: truth depends upon fact, which is true "independently" of its being believed. This stance, of course, forces us to make a distinction between what a man believes, and what makes his belief true.

Our third conclusion is based on this premise: while it is the fact which makes my belief true, the fact, as the embodiment of truth must be experienced by the mind before it is actualized as belief.

When fact is actualized as belief, belief becomes the same thing as knowledge.

Certitude

To ask the question what is truth? is to ask what is certainty? To possess truth is to be certain of its existence, and aware of the ability of the mind to apprehend, by degrees, its meaningfulness. This implies there are degrees of the apprehension of certainty, but we would not agree with Zenophanes in his insistence there are degrees of truth-likeness. Moreover, we are not certain if we agree with Ayer who says it is possible to be completely sure of something which is in fact true, but yet not to know it. We are puzzled by the words *to know it*. If he means to know it absolutely (in its entirety, and as an absolute) his position is correct. Is there an existent which the mind can know absolutely? If this were true, it would make of mind first cause. To be certain is the absence of doubt as to the existence of the reality of truth.

Chapter Five: The Epistemological Stance of Giveness

The relationship of certitude to truth is apparent. The steps needed to be taken by the mind to attain or reach this certainty is not so apparent.

And, then, there is the problem of probability. Is it true, for instance, that the mind cannot consider the potentiality of probability unless there are basic certainties? If so, what are these certainties? How does one determine potentiality in probability? Or, another question which confronts us. Is it true that only what is certain can be known?

Our answer to the above questions rests upon one premise. Whatever is known, as certainty, truth, or even its potentiality, is known *via* ideas. Here is one point on which we agree with Hume. He tells us that all certainty arises from the comparison of ideas, and from the discovery of such relations as are unalterable so long as the ideas continue the same.

The epistemological process, regardless of its dimensions, is the embodiment of the cognitive act, or mental adventure. Even if we say: "I know because I feel it" is to say the mind is using a language which gives expression to our sensate reaction, and language is the voice of ideas. Regis, in quoting St. Thomas, takes the same position by saying that certitude exists in two ways in a thing; by essence and by participation. It exists by essence in the cognitive power and by participation in everything which is infallibly moved towards its end by the cognitive power.

What is this end? It is perfect certainty. Dewey calls it complete certainty, and this, he says, can be fulfilled in pure knowing alone. He does, however, refer to effect certainty and this is what man wants. What man wants is determined by the ideas which he has about what he wants. This makes certitude functional only on the level of consciousness, and, as Weigel and Madden would like to add, on the level of metaphysical intuition because the real is assimilated in itself, and since certitude is nothing but the tranquillity of truth achievement, the certitude is here inevitable.

Chapter Five: The Epistemological Stance of Giveness

But, if it is not inevitable? What about imperfect or prudential certitude? Weigel and Madden have two things to say about this in their discussion on Descartes. First, prudential certitude as achieved on other levels is a true certitude but of a different order. This certitude makes science and history possible, and it must not be considered as a poor relation. Second, prudential certitude accompanies a spontaneous assent of the knowing faculty on the empirical or faith plane, when no positive motive is given to withhold assent. Such an assent is subsequently reformable; it will never be entirely wrong. The justification of such assent is double; (a) on the plane of action which is necessary for life some assent is needed; (b) the knowing faculty is of itself capable of achieving the real and its spontaneous activity is in accord with its intuited movement toward truth. Working spontaneously and naturally it will reach the truth at least by approximation.

Drawing together these thoughts, what are the premises upon which we develop cognitive certitude? They number four.

1. The will orders and provides the direction for the intellect.

2. The mind orders and provides the cognitive energy for the operant principles which direct the knowing power found in certitude.

3. There are degrees of certitude which run parallel to the degrees of the apprehension of truth.

4. Since knowledge bespeaks conclusions, and conclusions imply an integration of detail, the mind, working by means of its cognitive operant principles achieves certitude when the intellect functions as an integrative power, relating fact to fact and determining the relationships which alone provides closure for a whole.

Affirmation

In our search for knowledge, we are on the constant lookout for basic evidence. Without it, knowledge cannot exist. This search implies consciousness. Affirmation is predicated on the assumption: consciousness exists.

Chapter Five: The Epistemological Stance of Giveness

While affirmation is based on consciousness, this does not tell us what it is. Hume has his answer. While he speaks of affirmation in the universal sense, his thought is applicable. He says that although we observe repeated instances of similar sequences, no finite number of such observations can by themselves justify a universal affirmation.

We are interested in his word justify. What justifies affirmation? The answer is causal beliefs. Here is our reasoning.

How do we learn? How do we know? Here are questions the epistemologist is not alone in asking. To know requires the cognitive ingenuity both of an art and science. The moment we say that knowing is an art as well as a science there is the implication that the mind is aware of its need to appraise, at all times, what it is doing. It is mind evaluating its own criteria for the determination of the actualization of its prime objective, the establishment of truth. These criteria, the mind realizes, must be delineated as well as defined. Affirmation enters as an integrative force in the intellective process because of its basic premise, namely, that truth is personalized by mind through experiencing its meaning. Affirmation is the act by which meaning is accepted as truth for that particular mind.

Doubt

Doubt is an existent because error is real. The greater the possibility of error, greater is the potentiality for doubt.

The Source of Doubt

The source of doubt is an insufficiency of knowledge. When the mind does not possess enough knowledge about its object, questions arise; the implications are here: the material of knowledge is not sufficient to validate means for the actualization of the real. The mind acts and reacts according to the directives inherent in its reasoning process; when there is a lack of ground on which to function, there is hesitation, the methodical step slows, doubt darkens the cognitive horizon.

Chapter Five: The Epistemological Stance of Giveness

The mind is engaged in a constant struggle; it never relaxes in its search for truth. In this quest, the mind is aware that truth supplies its own evidence; to find this evidence and actualize its meaning, is to realize truth. What is not evidential, must be determined by the mind and declared invalid. It is when the mind neglects this task that doubt comes into being.

The investigation of reality is the sole responsibility of the mind. Since what is real is real only because of the reality of its cause, it is cause which is the starting point of the investigation. The inquiry must continue until all questions of doubt have been satisfactorily answered. Doubt is an active agent in the intellectual process; it is constantly raising questions about the apparency of reality. Questions, of course, raise objections. To overcome an objection requires an understanding of cause. It is in cause along the mind finds the reasons for differences in what is real.

Objections are strange intellectualized parings. The mind raises objections and so does its objects. The objective of the mind is truth; since truth supplies its own evidence, opposing evidence posits objections, realizable, of course, by the mind. Doubt is always methodical in the kinds of questions it raises; its objections are natural corollaries to insufficient and inadequate evidence. Doubt suggests that the mind has been partially blinded by its own empirically imposed methodological strictures. This is to say, the mind often fails to comprehend the potentiality of the evidence already supplied by reality. In this way, the mind causes the self to doubt its own inquisite techniques because of its failure to answer the objections posited by existing evidence. Methodologies fail when the mind fails to determine the relationship between evidence and the principles underlying cause for the material of knowledge. Principles precede the methodology of which it exposes content. This tenet the mind experiences when it asks questions about the nature of being in order to comprehend it as truth. Doubt is destroyed as an existent when being is realized as being. This does not imply that doubt is a necessary ingredient of the intellectual

Chapter Five: The Epistemological Stance of Giveness

process. However, it can serve as a braking factor, a mode of caution suggesting a more highly developed deliberateness in analytical technique.

Clarification is the mind's substitute for doubt. Certainty is the only means of dispelling the possibility of error, the grounds for doubt. Certainty draws conclusions known by the mind because they are based on the principles underlying the causality of evidential premises.

Cause is evident truth in every conclusion validated by the mind. Doubt cannot exist in such a setting.

Doubt According to Descartes, St. Thomas and Kant

We begin with Descartes; his concern is with self-evident truth; knowledge possesses, he says, a foundation "which would be impregnable to doubt." And yet, "Descartes' method of systematic doubt... is a method of destroying all false prejudices of the mind, in order to arrive at the unshakable basis of self-evident truth."

Here is an epistemologist who chooses to use doubt as a method of actualizing truth; his reason for doing so is evident. Error, as well as truth is an existent. Therefore, he is confronted with the need to determine criteria of truth. There is a quest here; it is the mode by which the mind discovers truth through errorless knowledge. It is a matter of discovering error as well as actualizing truth. Error gives rise to doubt; the mind is dependent upon reason and its processes to articulate all factors which create doubt because of existing error. In error, there is one reality dimension missing from its being; there is the failure to connect one dependency assumption with another. In determining the relationship between facts, such relationships depend upon underlying assumptions. If these are missing, error exists, and doubt arises. Descartes doubted everything which would make room for doubt. For him, the mind must not be deceived. The way the mind is deceived is for it to substitute error for truth. To doubt until the mind ascertains truth is to discover truth. It is a methodical doubt, of which

Chapter Five: The Epistemological Stance of Giveness

he speaks, a doubt whose quest is understanding.

The mind is deceived when it lacks evidence in its material of knowledge. Both Descartes and St. Thomas ascribe to this statement. "St. Thomas defines doubt as the impossibility of deciding upon one contradictory, as a mind vacillating between two alternatives, one of which destroys the other, and refusing its assent through fear of error."

Kant was also concerned about the question of evidence *in* the material of knowledge. He saw it in terms of the reality factor, the nature of which must be considered as primary datum. It is the methodology inherent in the reasoning process (which gives no place to doubt) that permits the primary datum to give an explanation of its own being. Thus, there is no place for doubt to originate.

While these men may differ, and in great detail, if we were to analyze their total positions in this matter (in such areas as will, intellect and assent), there is a point of common agreement: when there is a lack of evidence in its material knowledge, the mind cannot function with certitude.

Without certitude, there can be only doubt.

CHAPTER SIX
THE REALITY OF THE CONCEPT

The Concept

The human mind cannot know if it is unable to conceptualize. Knowledge cannot exist without concepts.

The Instrument of Interpretation

The concept is the instrument of interpretation. The principles of conceptualization make it possible for meaning to be brought into being; meaning is the resultant of the empirically based, interpretative function, of the intellectual process. The concept is the empirically tested attitude of the intellect.

Concepts are a mind concept. Meaning reveals itself by means of the concept; to experience the concept is to experience meaning. On the other hand, it is the concept which permits the mind to experience. All of this action takes place by the mind and within the mind.

The intriguing thing about the concept is its power of interpretation. Perhaps a better substitute for the word power would be energy. The concept possesses a self-actualizing energy which feeds upon (and thus renews itself) the potentiality and positivity of the idea. It is the concept which interprets the meaningfulness of experience for the mind. The functioning mind demands a logic in its actions; it requires a methodical progression in the development of its experience. It is the concept that tells us the material of experience becomes the content of the mind; the intellect has the responsibility of ordering the meaningful effects realizable in experience. The concept provides the correlation between connectives in the interpretative process of developing the potentiality of the idea. Every idea possesses qualities; to determine the

Chapter Six: The Reality of the Concept

nature of the relationships between qualities, and the causal principles underlying these connectives, is to put your finger on the source of energy basic in the realization of the experiential potential of the concept.

For the concept, the most important things which exist are the qualities of the idea. To conceptualize quality is to correlate the principles which relate one fact to another. In this way the concept is the means by which the mind structures reality; it is the way in which the intention of reality is discovered; in effect, it is the criterion of experience. This position puts to flight Kant's position when he says that it is a mere tautology to speak of general or common concepts. He would have noted an inconsistency here in his stand if he had considered the empirical implications of another of his questions. He stated the question in the form of a proposition: one cannot deduce anything from a concept other than that which the concept contains.

The concept is always propositional in nature. Without this characteristic of its nature, its interpretative powers would be meaningless. Propositions concern themselves with the problems found in interpretation; a chief anxiety is with the whole question of validation. This pertains to the relationships between components in experience. Experience itself is a fusion process; there are no stages or breaks; rather, components, as acts, fuse with one another and become the embodiment of experience. To validate one component in relation to another is the task of the proposition. Propositions evolve from concepts. Knowledge builds on knowledge; it is the concept which acts as the adhesive, joining one building block to the next. Validation always raises the question of critique. Naturally, it is our concern here, as well. Throughout his theory of knowledge, Kant, likewise, worked with this problem. Critique suggests analysis; how then, does one analyze a concept? He says, by content. The content of the concept is given *a priori*. Moreover, he labels this as notions. Insofar as analysis is concerned, it must include a dissection of the faculty of understanding itself, in order to investigate the possibility of concepts *a*

Chapter Six: The Reality of the Concept

priori by looking for them in the understanding alone as their birthplace, and by analyzing the pure use of this faculty. Kant continues. We shall therefore follow up the pure concepts to their first seeds and dispositions in the human understanding in which they lie prepared, until on the occasion of experience they are developed and by the same understanding are exhibited in their purity, freed from the empirical conditions attaching to them.

This is quite different from St. Thomas' position. We recall that an important relationship for him in this context was between concept and principle. He defined them in his characteristic way in terms of object and objective knowledge. In this way he tells us that the concept is more than a mental word. Moreover, it is more than just a reaction to an object. The concept is the assurance carried by the mind that the process of intellection is functioning.

Deciding What is Real

The mind is real; as a reality, it must decide what else is real. This it does through its process of intellection.

The concept is real; as a reality, it has the task of assisting sense perception to decide what is fact. There is no question; the mind uses the concept to form its judgments. It is an integral part of the understanding; it helps the mind decide what is real. To prove its function, the mind subjects the concept to empirical tests.

To Test the Concept

There is but one way the validity of the concept can be tested, and that is *via* its implications. Concepts are experiential in nature; they evolve from experience, and they themselves experience. Such action is not without its implications. The test is one for logicality. The governing question is, how logical is the experience which has evolved from experience? This is the same as asking, how logically structured is the concept? Has the concept become something more than a notion? There is nothing Kantian about these questions. The tester of the

Chapter Six: The Reality of the Concept

concept is truth; and since truth is actualized only in its relation to experienced fact, its implications for the concept are readily apparent. The implications of truth and the implications of the concept meet on the testing ground of experiential conditions. The function of the concept is governed by the experiential values inherent within its implications for learning.

A concept is not an entity; concepts evolve from experience. Since the concept is used by the mind, the mind is constantly testing for cogency; it must determine the applicability of its laws. The mind perseveres in its insistence that the concept becomes self-evident in the thought process. When it does become self-evident, it has been recognized in the intellectual process as an ordered whole. Only as an ordered whole can the concept function as a criterion of reality. "Logically considered, the concept is perception congealed into knowledge; in the judgment and in perception we gain in the concept and in knowledge we possess the truth." (Windelband)

The human mind thinks with concepts; it thinks as it experiences the implications of its thought. In this way the mind realizes the relationships which exist in experience. What lies beyond the concept, therefore beyond experience, can have no meaning.

Presuppositions

The theory of knowledge is dependent, for its intellective movement, upon a pivotal concept: the nature and responsibility of presuppositions. In order to learn, we first must inquire about the potentiality inherent in the object of our knowledge. However, the direction of the inquiry, as well as its methodological stance, is dependent upon a factor which must be decided upon before the inquiry begins. This is where the presupposition is brought into action, its nature determined, and its responsibility validated.

On his way toward learning, the learner posits assumptions, or, as I prefer to call them, working hypotheses. The mind cannot function

Chapter Six: The Reality of the Concept

unless it has something on which to work. It is experience which provides the mind with its propositions. Since the mind is determined to believe something, it uses these propositions in this capacity until it has proven them false. Presuppositions are assumed truths posited for the sake of initiating the intellective process and determining the potentiality of its propositions which remain to be validated.

Presuppositions are more than apperceptions. Apperceptions are one part of the construct of presuppositions. As a matter of fact, they serve in a way which makes the presupposition an epistemological functionary. We disagree with Kant when he says that apperception is the presupposition of having and using concepts, and is therefore not itself a concept. Apperception is a concept, it is the only concept which is able to conceptualize. Apperception is the presupposition functioning through its process of conceptualization.

The presupposition must conceptualize; without this process there would be no propositions, and the mind is unable to function without them. What we are saying is that the mind has some knowledge of the essence of its presuppositions. Without this knowledge, presuppositions would be meaningless and without direction; the mind refuses to move on meaningless directives.

Principles

The only entity which exists is an absolute. A fact is not an entity because it is not an absolute; it is dependent upon other facts for its existence. Principles underlie the relationships which exist between facts. These principles determine the nature of the relationships, as well as the potentiality inherent in the fact. Essentially, principles are empirically based working hypotheses. The responsibility of principles is to validate the relationships referred to above. Principles evolve from the law of universal causation.

Validation is the pivotal concept in an understanding of principles. How does one justify the use of principles, as well as validate their use, in the process of intellection? To know is to make certain assertions; inferences abound; so then, what are the justifying norms by which the knowledge gained can be empirically validated?

All of this might imply that we come to know principles by means different than that for facts. This is not true. To know means the subject has actualized its object and experienced its meaning. This is true whether the object is a fact or a principle. There is a proposition in both fact and principle, and both must be experienced to be known.

There is a need in the mind to legitimatize its knowledge. Descartes recognized this; he would agree with our question, how do we know what we know, and why? What are the working hypotheses, the principles, which enable us to logically connect and thus validate what we know with its cause? Here is the penetrating effect of the principle at work in the hypothesis.

Categories of Principles

St. Thomas gives us the historical picture of principles and their categories.

The ancients, in fact, discovered three categories of principles, of which the first unifies the multiplicity of local movements, the second unifies the becoming of things from within, and the third unifies this same becoming from without. The latter categories include the four causes, which are unifying principles in the respective domains of matter, form efficiency, and finality. Furthermore, considered in relation to their effects, or to the diversity they unify, these four causes give rise to twelve different ways of being first principles, *i.e.,* of being the unifying form of a multitude.

First Principles

It is these "ways" of being first principles which interest us in this connection; "being the unifying form of a multitude" supplies the introduction necessary for understanding the role of first principles.

Chapter Six: The Reality of the Concept

First principles are absolutes defined as cause. What exists evolves from cause, and depends upon cause for its meaning. First principles serve as the source of logic; from this source order evolves. First principles serve as the intellective structure of the laws of thought and of causality. In this capacity they provide the basis of knowledge. They are more than definitions; in Whitehead's terminology, they are the modes of thought itself. All knowledge must be deduced from first principles. This is saying no more than all existents evolve from cause and depend upon cause to be known.

First principles are the embodiment of truth; the principles reflect the premises upon which causal truth operates. First principles are the intellection of what is necessary in cause; their authority is independent of that which they serve; they are being itself. First principles then, are causal principles. What must be remembered in the process of intellection is that what is known is only fully known when the causal principle (which first confronted the learner with the object) is known. This is to say, we know a fact only when its dependency upon other facts is realized, and the principles which unite the facts are actualized by the mind. The causal principle joins the knower and the known.

Propositions

It is Dewey's and Bentley's position that a proposition may be almost anything; it consists commonly of "terms" but terms, even while being the "insides" of propositions, may be either words or non-verbal "things." This is a unique way of saying that the expressional essence of the proposition is language, the being of terms. It also tells us that whatever is, may serve as the being of a confrontation, the essence of an existent. Therefore, whatever is, may confront the mind as a proposition. But, whatever is, needs a mind to react, via language, to its projected being. This is the most adequate way of defining a proposition.

For Wittgenstein, to define a proposition is to understand it, and this means, he says, to know what is the case if it is true. I strongly

Chapter Six: The Reality of the Concept

suspect this is a stronger position than Woozley's when he contends that to find meaning in a proposition is to find meaning in a sentence. Woozley's position is stronger than Wittgenstein's if he insists that each proposition is a datum. Perhaps Wittgenstein implies this, for, is it possible to understand something which is not a datum? If we were to ask Russell to enter the discussion at this point he would undoubtedly say that a proposition which is not a datum may derive credibility from various different sources. But, where does this leave us: Russell explains his position. He insists that it is not possible to make propositions the ultimate subject-matter of inquiry. This position is explained in so far as he feels that his problem here has been throughout the relation between events and the propositions that they cause men to assert. Thus, he does not regard things as the object of inquiry, since he holds them to be a metaphysical delusion.

In spite of the foregoing explanation, he hardly handles, to our satisfaction, the paradox of his statement when he suggests that a proposition may not be a datum. We find a number of implications for this proposition about a proposition in a statement of Russell's quoted by Farber. "The proof that the contradictory of some proposition is self-contradictory is likely to require other principles of deduction besides the law of contradiction." To this, Farber replies: In any case, the reflexive method is intended to present us with a number of principles which must be accepted in some form as unavoidable presuppositions in any system of rational discourse.

Guzie is not at all satisfied with a position like the one advanced by Russell. There is another side to this canvas, he insists. Corresponding to the philosophical aim of reasoning to the ontological causes of activity are propositions, he says, consisting of ontological knowledge — knowledge, that is, in which the object is revealed through experiential induction in such a way that sensory evidences and observable behavioral patterns are subservient to the direct intelligibility implied by the being's activity. Definitions and judgments, he continues, are thus made in terms of the principles of

Chapter Six: The Reality of the Concept

being and its various analogous classifications. Individual concepts are also ontological in form, in that they express aspects of the object as it is in reality.

This "in reality" of Guzie reminds us of Hume's stance: "In reality, there is scarcely a proposition in Euclid so simple as not to consist of more parts than are to be found in any moral reasoning which runs not into chimera and conceit." Hume explains this statement by saying that it seems a proposition which will not admit of much dispute that all our ideas are nothing but copies of our impressions; or, in other words, that it is impossible for us to think of anything which we have not antecedently felt, either by our external or internal senses.

In Anticipation of Experience

Hawkins responds to Hume by means of the position of R. E. Hobart. He tells us that Hobart manages to derive a positive theory from Hume by abandoning the demand that propositions should be either evident or demonstrable. This is explained in this way. Appearances of fact are ultimate, and we ask proof for them only when faced with conflicting appearances. The principle of inductive generalization, however it is to be formulated, is an ultimate and unchallenged appearance of fact. Even if we wanted to hold that no appearance was trustworthy without proof, this would itself be a generalization from experience and could not cast doubt on the principle by which we generalize from experience. Hence this principle is unassailable. Here we must say that the theory of knowledge involved is unacceptable. It is not true that everything that I can suppose to be possible is taken as fact unless there is contrary evidence. Nothing is an appearance of fact unless there is contrary evidence. Nothing is an appearance of fact unless there is at least probable evidence for it, and, since probability is always dependent on evidence, the probable depends in the end on the evidently true. We are right therefore, he says, in looking for evidence for the inductive principle, and no positive theory can be built upon it in the absence of evidence.

Chapter Six: The Reality of the Concept

The word evidence is at the forefront of our thinking at this point. Is evidence to be equated with factual content? If so, Ayer says that all propositions which have factual content are empirical hypotheses, and that the function of an empirical hypothesis is to provide a rule for the anticipation of experience. This means that every empirical hypothesis must be relevant to some actual, or possible, experience, so that a statement which is not relevant to any experience is not an empirical hypothesis, and accordingly has no factual content. But, he says, this is precisely what the principle of verifiability asserts.

What is this principle of verifiability? Polanyi asks to be heard. We have seen, he says, that the propositions embodied in natural science are not derived by any definite rule from the data of experience. They are first arrived at by a form of guessing based on premises which are by no means inescapable and cannot even be clearly defined; after which they are verified by a process of observational hardening which always gives play to the scientist's personal judgment. In every judgment of scientific validity there thus remains implied the supposition that we accept the premises of science and that the scientist's conscience can be relied upon.

What are these premises as they relate only to the proposition?

Propositions as Premises

Russell answers our question. Propositions, he says, which are premises for empirical knowledge are fundamental for any empirical theory of knowledge. He supports this contention by saying when a proposition concerning a particular matter of fact is inferred, there must always be among the premises other matters of fact from which some general law is obtained by induction. It is therefore impossible, he states, that all our knowledge of matters of fact should be inferred. In turn, he strengthens this position by contending that given any systematic body of propositions, such as it contained in some science in which there are general laws, it is possible, usually in an indefinite number of ways, to pick out certain of the propositions as premises, and

Chapter Six: The Reality of the Concept

deduce the remainder.

This question of inference is one which cannot be ignored. It raises a question often by-passed by epistemologists; is there a mind-stance different in the cognitive set in its totality which is not present in the inferential process? Perhaps we must ask it in this way. Are propositions independent of mind? Rather, does not the proposition require a mind in order to be a proposition? Perhaps this is the same as asking: does truth depend upon another mind? Does this imply that truth itself is inferential and the proposition is but the means of conveyance of its essence and meaning?

If the proposition is mind dependent, then we must take a look at the intellect in this connection.

The Judgmental Assent of the Intellect

To answer the above question, we use a number of propositions of Guzie, but recast them into questions. Only in this manner will we be enabled to penetrate to the core of our problem. Are propositions but symbols of the real facts they represent? Are the things to which the intellect judgmentally assent themselves directly intelligible? Is it correct to say that once the intellect actively directs its attention to the immediate facts of sense experience, it assents to them without any further reasoning? Is it impossible to reason logically to the direct intelligibility of sense experience?

Here, again, we are confronted with the problem of inference in relation to the proposition. It may stand us in good stead, at least in reference to our reasoning process, if we listen to Hume; without doubt he is speaking to us. You say, he says, that the one proposition is an inference from the other; but you must confess that the inference is not intuitive, neither is it demonstrative. Of what nature is it then? To say it is experimental is begging the question. For all inferences from experience suppose, as their foundation, that the future will resemble the past and that similar powers will be conjoined with similar sensible

Chapter Six: The Reality of the Concept

qualities. If there be any suspicion that the course of nature may change, and that the past may be no rule for the future, all experience becomes useless and can give use to no inference or conclusion. It is impossible, therefore, that any arguments from experience can prove this resemblance of the past to the future, since all these arguments are founded on the supposition of that resemblance.

Farber agrees by saying that propositions about the future involve possibility; various alternatives appear to be capable of realization from the perspective of our present knowledge.

If experience is useless for the future, wherein lies the need for verification? We are tempted to ask, in addition to the above, whether or not what cannot be verified must be labeled as meaningless? If something is experienced, is it possible for it to be meaningless? Ayer wants us to believe that a proposition is said to be verifiable if, and only if, its truth could be conclusively established in experience.

And how is this to be accomplished? In establishing the premise that all propositions are relational.

A Relation is Predicated on the Referent

The above is a statement of Hawkins, for he tells us that all propositions are relational; all exhibit a unity in difference, and all possess a subject and a predicate, for a relation is predicated of the referent. While Leibniz contends that the only way we can define substance is by way of making a total of its predicates, he, too, realizes this forces him into the position of insisting that every proposition has a subject and a predicate.

If a relation is predicated of the referent, then Farber is selling the right idea of Kant when he says that a proposition is synthetic (is said to be) if the predicate adds something to the subject and analytic if the predicate is contained in the subject. But what about propositions referring to subjective states? Is this equally true of propositions with objective reference? Whitehead raises the same question in his

Chapter Six: The Reality of the Concept

proposition, the logical subjects of a proposition supply the element of given-ness requisite for truth and falsehood. But does all of this suggest that a proposition is self-evident in itself, if its predicate is contained in the notion of subject?" St. Thomas answers our question: "certain axioms or propositions are universally self-evident to all; and such are the propositions whose terms are known to all, as, every whole is greater than its parts, and, things equal to one and the same are equal to each other."

The Proposition versus the Sentence

Reread the preceding paragraph. Did you make a distinction between propositions and sentences? Is there a distinction which can be drawn between the two? Woozley seems to think so. A proposition, he says,

> is normally distinguished from a sentence by saying that a sentence is a form of words combined according to the grammatical and syntactical rules of the language to which the sentence belongs, while a proposition is not a form of words at all, but is what the sentence means.

> He defends this position by adding: a proposition, then, "is different, on the one hand, from any of the variety of sentences, written or spoken, in which it may be expressed, and, on the other hand, from the events which it purports to describe, and which makes it true or false."

Now, reread the paragraph alluded to above. Is it not begging the question to even suggest that a proposition is not a sentence? Or, perhaps this is not our real problem. We hastily answer, it is not. Our real interest lies in Woozley's last statement: "...and which makes it true or false."

If a Proposition is True

If a proposition is true, what makes it so?

Chapter Six: The Reality of the Concept

Since we have been critical of Woozley, perhaps we are under obligation to hear him out, at least, as he reacts to other positions taken to our problem. We are taking the freedom to restructure a number of his statements, and recasting them as questions.

Is it possible to discover a proposition and declare it true by observing the facts? Is there such a thing as observing the facts? Under scrutiny, when we think we are observing facts, is this always the case? Certain propositions, if formulated, are they necessarily true? It is possible to formulate propositions ex hypothesi? (Woozley)

This last question serves as a pivotal point in our discussion, so we must permit him to answer it. There are no minds to do the job, he says, but that does not affect the truth (or otherwise) of the statement that if they were formulated they would be true. (Woozley)

We have now come full circle in our argument. And yet, there are barbed questions which continue to disturb our epistemological ease, such as:

Can we ever know whether the proposition which one believes true, is satisfied? Especially in the case of purported factual knowledge, is it not always logically possible that future data, data which one does not and cannot have at the time of one's judgment, will turn out to be disconfirming? (Blackstone)

Is the best one can say, then, "that a given factual proposition is highly probable"?

Is it necessary that later propositions should be "logically deducible from earlier ones"?

What is necessary is that "the earlier ones should supply whatever ground exist for thinking it likely that the later ones are true" (Russell). Russell enhances this proposition by saying: when we are considering empirical knowledge, the earliest propositions in the hierarchy, which give the grounds for all the others, are not deduced from other propositions, and yet are not mere arbitrary assumptions. They have

Chapter Six: The Reality of the Concept

grounds, though their grounds are not propositions, but observed occurrences. Hence, we are confronted here with a question asked earlier.

These propositions Russell calls "basic propositions." Does Russell equate grounds with form? If so, we could agree with St. Thomas that in order for

> a proposition to be true it suffices that the predicate agree with the subject in some way. But in order that a proposition be true *per se* the predicate must agree with the subject by reason of the form of the subject.

Once again, the circle is closed. But, satisfactorily? Only partially. Closure will be complete when the mind has recast the following questions, making of them true propositions.

A Priori **Propositions**

Is it possible for a true *a priori* proposition to be false?

Does the difference between *a priori* and empirical propositions lie in our mode of establishing them?

Once we grasp the truth of an *a priori* proposition, is it necessary to look for further evidence in its favor? And, do we treat fresh instances or applications of it as evidence at all?

How does one emphasize the necessity of *a priori* propositions and the contingency of empirical propositions? By emphasizing the distinction between *a priori* and empirical propositions by means of its relevance to the supposed difference in kind between knowledge and belief?

How is the validity of *a priori* propositions determined? What criterion is used to determine the validity of empirical propositions? (Ayer)

Is the purpose of a theory of truth to describe the criteria by which the validity of the various kinds of propositions is determined? (Ayer)

Chapter Six: The Reality of the Concept

Analytic Propositions

Is there a sense in which analytic propositions give us new knowledge? Do analytic propositions always call attention to linguistic usages, and reveal unsuspected implications in our assertions and beliefs? (Ayer)

Basic Propositions

May basic propositions be defined as those propositions about particular occurrences which, after a critical scrutiny, may still be believed independently of any extraneous evidence in their favor? (Russell)

Even though there may be evidence in favor of a basic proposition, is it this evidence alone that causes our belief? (Russell)

Must a basic proposition be known independently of inference from other propositions, but not independently of evidence? (Russell)

Must there be a perceptive occurrence which gives the cause and is considered to give the reason for believing the basic proposition? (Russell)

Is it possible, from a logical point of view, so to analyze our empirical knowledge that its primitive propositions (apart from logic and generalities) should all have been, at the moment when they were first believed, basic propositions? (Russell)

Is there a requirement which says that basic propositions should not contradict each other, and makes it desirable, if possible, to give them a logical form which makes mutual contradiction impossible? (Russell)

Are there other properties than these that a basic proposition should possess: (1) it must be caused by some sensible occurrence; (2) it must be of such a form that no other basic proposition can contradict it? (Russell)

Chapter Six: The Reality of the Concept

The Composition of a Proposition

Is the composition of a proposition the work of nature or of reason and intellect? (St. Thomas)

Empirical Propositions

Empirical propositions, except when their subject-matter happens to be linguistic, are true *only* in virtue of occurrences which are not linguistic? (Russell)

Existential Propositions

Is Kant correct when he says that every reasonable person must admit that all existential propositions are synthetic?

Are all existential propositions contingent because all existential propositions are synthetic?

The Factual Proposition

Is there a sense in which it can be said that a given factual proposition is always true if it is once really true?

The False Proposition

What are the implications inherent in Russell's position that a false proposition of any kind involves all the other propositions, whether true or false?

The General Proposition

Is it possible to know a general proposition without knowing "any instance of it"?

Hume has pointed out that no general proposition whose validity is subject to the test of actual experience can ever be logically certain. Using Ayer's mind here as the means for recasting a proposition, is there the possibility that the general proposition will be confuted on some future occasion, regardless of how often it is verified in practice?

Chapter Six: The Reality of the Concept

The Genuine Proposition

Ayer helps us to think through the preceding statements, by permitting us to raise yet others.

Are all genuine propositions limited to two classes, namely, in the terminology of Hume, those concerned with "relations of ideas," and those which concern "matters of fact"?

Do the genuine propositions which concern "relations of ideas" comprise the *a priori* propositions of logic and pure mathematics? If so, are they necessary and certain only because they are analytic? Is the reason why these propositions cannot be refuted in experience because they do not make any assertion about the empirical world, but simply record our determination to use symbols in a certain fashion?

Or, are propositions concerning empirical matters of fact hypotheses which can be probable but never certain? Are we able to explain the nature of truth when we have given an account of the method of their validation? (Ayer)

The Logic of Propositions

What are the implications of Russell's position that the logic of propositions is the study of the laws in accordance with which combinations are formed with the conjunctions if, and, or, and the negative not? (Poincare)

Memory Propositions

In admitting memory propositions among factual premises, are we conceding that our premises may be doubtful and sometimes false? (Russell)

The Metaphysical Proposition

If a metaphysical proposition is a proposition claiming truth, is it, by its very nature, exempt from any operational test? (Childe)

Chapter Six: The Reality of the Concept

The Philosophical Proposition

What are the inherent implicative values in Russell's statement that philosophical propositions must be *a priori?* Does this imply that they can be neither proved nor disproved by empirical evidence?

Scientific Propositions

Are scientific propositions operational or functional rather than essential? Do such functional laws necessarily involve the hypothetical method, if they are to be experimentally revealed as the best laws? (Guzie)

It is necessary for all scientific propositions to be read strictly in the light of the selectively abstracted data involved? (Guzie)

Are there scientific propositions which do not refer definitely to any observable facts, but rather describe something real which may manifest itself in many indefinite ways? Does this imply that there exists therefore no explicit rules by which a scientific proposition can be obtained from observational data? Must we therefore also accept that no explicit rules can exist to decide whether to uphold or abandon any scientific proposition in face of any particular new observation? Is this to supply clues for the apprehension of reality? That is, the process underlying scientific discovery? Does the apprehension of reality thus gained, form, in turn, a clue to future observations? Is it the process underlying verification? In both processes, is there involved an intuition of the relation between observation and reality? Is it a faculty which can range over all grades of sagacity, from the highest level present in the inspired guesses of scientific genius, down to a minimum required for ordinary perception? Does verification, even though usually more subject to rules than discovery, rest ultimately on mental powers which go beyond the application of any definite rules? (Polanyi)

Synthetic Propositions

Are all synthetic propositions empirical hypotheses? Is speculative

Chapter Six: The Reality of the Concept

knowledge of two distinct kinds, that which relates to questions of empirical fact, and that which relates to questions of value? Are "statements of value" genuine synthetic propositions? Is it possible for "statements of value" to be represented as hypotheses which are used to predict the course of our sensations? (Ayer)

The Truth of Propositions

Is it possible to discover the truth of a proposition by observing the facts and by detecting the correspondence between proposition and fact? (Woozley)

Does every true proposition logically depend on all other true propositions, and that no proposition can then be completely and absolutely true unless one knows all the others? (Woozley)

Is it necessary for a proposition's truth to depend not merely on its relationship of entailment with other propositions, but also on what those other propositions are, *i.e.,* on whether or not they are independently acceptable? (Woozley)

Universal Propositions

Do universal propositions, based on perception alone, apply only to a definite period of time? Can they tell us anything about what happens at other times? Does the whole practical utility of knowledge depend upon its power of foretelling the future? (Russell)

Are universal propositions drawn from experience contingent and problematic unless they have some prior warrant? Is it true that knowledge which is certain cannot be grounded in the particulars of experience if it is to apply to particular experiences in advance? Does it only come from the possession of some universal by which the particular is implied? Can these universals be reached by generalization? Are there universal truths which are known otherwise than through experience? Can such universal propositions be logically derived unless from other such universals as premises? Must there be some universal truths which are first premises logically underived and

Chapter Six: The Reality of the Concept

representing an original knowledge from which we start? Must such propositions be axiomatic and self-evident? (Lewis)

Reality

What is real? Is there a more important question the learner could ask than this one? We doubt it. To determine reality is to know the essence of existence. This is the reason our problem is epistemological in nature.

Perhaps another way of asking the question would be, what should the learner see in reality? Steenberghen tells us that Heraclitus saw only multiplicity and movement in reality, while Parmenides and Zeno ignored becoming and the multiple in favor of the identical and unchangeable. Plato, of course, was greatly enamored with the question. He was concerned with the relationship between reality and the subjective image which the learner has of it. His question rests on the existence or non-existence of reality. Moreover, he was faced with the problem of fitting reality into categories. Are categories existent empirical realities? Perhaps Aristotle was correct after all.

Is this image of which Plato speaks the same as the similarities of which Locke speaks? Locke tells us that everything real is individual, but that there are similarities in nature. Hawkins criticizes Locke by pointing out that he supposes there must be a special kind of mental object to serve as a universal idea.

For Kant, reality means fact-hood. This is an exact translation, says Heidegger. The word is *Sachheit,* and he says it alludes to the quiddity (Wasgehalt) of the essent which is delimited through essentia.

But it is Bergson who strikes at the heart of our problem. In his *Creative Evolution* he speaks of the Greek mind, and for that mind, the reality which is the object of the truest knowledge is found in some privileged moment when a process of change attains its climactic apogee.

Is reality the object of knowledge? If reality is *only* the object of

Chapter Six: The Reality of the Concept

knowledge, does this imply that knowledge itself is not real? To raise these questions means that we are thinking about reality; isn't thinking itself the substance of reality? To be able to think implies that something or someone is thinking. Would we want to say at this point in our discussion that reality is what is? Or, do we want to imply that what is exists because of its potentiality? This is what Polanyi wants us to believe. The real for him is that which is expected to reveal itself indeterminately in the future. Hence an explicit statement can bear on reality only by virtue of the tacit coefficient associated with it. (Polanyi)

There is a potentiality inherent in what is. The *is* is a matter of the becoming of reality; it is this factor which makes reality a truly creative process. What makes it creative is this. Reality not only is the object of knowledge, but it becomes the knowledge itself; it is the process of becoming which permits the mind to conceptualize its objects. We learn what is real by using what is real to actualize what *is*. This is the process of experiencing reality. In this sense the reality of an activity is creative when its potentiality is actualized; potentiality is realizable when knowledge is not considered an end, rather, as a creative means. The existentialist believes that knowledge, because of its reality factor, is a creative activity. Only in this way is it possible for reality to assume a meaningful role as an integral part of the process of intellection.

All of this tells us, then, reality not only is the object of cognitive activity, but the cognitive activity is as real as its object. This stance points out a fact we must not forget, namely, all knowledge is confined to human consciousness. This position does not disturb what we believe is the relativity of knowledge. Farber speaks to this when he says that reality is a complete domain at any given time because it comprises all events in space. But it is incomplete with respect to temporal development. He continues by saying that reality consists of a process of unique events which have a history, but which are all such that they have a spatiotemporal locus in physical reality.

Chapter Six: The Reality of the Concept

Bruno picks up this thought pattern and adds another dimension. Reality is a unitary process in which matter is both content and form. The essence of matter, he says, is the dynamic form that produces the infinite universe of species and individuals. In keeping with the position of Bruno, Cassirer strikes a responsive chord in our epistemological thinking when he says that reality is not a unique and homogeneous thing; it is immensely diversified, having as many different schemes and patterns as there are different organisms. Every organism is, so to speak, a monodic being. It has a world of its own because it has an experience of its own. It is this last sentence which provides us with a pivotal tenet for our discussion of reality.

What *is,* is real because it has an experience of its own. This is to say that it has a meaningfulness which is realizable by the human mind. It is reality which serves as the source of a causal principle underlying the relationships inherent in all thought processes. This does not imply a difference between truth and reality; but it does suggest that the mind apprehends, by degrees, the truth inherent in reality.

It is wrong to think that reality contains something, as load would have us believe. Reality contains, he says, if not all the objects and differences we know, at least the ground for all the objects and differences we know.

Reality *is;* it *is* because of its potential meaningfulness for the mind; it has experienced its cause, and realized the nature, scope and purpose of its essence. A container cannot function in a revelatory manner as suggested in the previous sentence, load is correct, however, when he discusses the view that reality is a unity, in all probability a mental unity, different aspects of which are known in different types of experience.

Our first conclusion in defining reality is this. Reality must be defined in causal terms; every existent is conditioned for existence. There is a reason (sufficient in nature) for what exists. This reason is found only in cause. To explain an existent is to find the explanation in the source of its being, in what is beyond the existent itself. We can say the same thing in this way. What is caused has a cause. The essence of what is caused evolves from its cause. Cause is real; what it causes is just as real as its source. Reality not only belongs to the existential order, but it is existence. What is actual is real. The essence of existence is the essence of reality; the mind refuses to believe that essence depends upon its potentiality for its reality.

The reality factor in epistemological theory is a given for experience; it exists to be known and experienced. Until it is known, its value for the learner remains relative. To experience it, the learner must perceive the structure of its qualities; because reality confronts the learner as an object, its construct is independent of the mind. But this independence does not preclude its nature (qualities) from becoming known. Lewis provides us with the epistemological adhesive needed here when he says that true knowledge is absolute because it conveys an absolute truth, though it can convey such truth only in relative terms.

It is a mistake, however, to even suggest that reality is no more than a given. In preceding paragraphs the most potent dimension of reality was discussed, namely, its potentiality. There is an abstract side to reality and this is its positivity; that is, the positivity of its potentiality. What we are saying is: potentiality is dependent upon and conditioned by its given. Potentiality is realizable by means of the intellective energy generated in the given. The given is an existent; whatever exists is real, not only because of what it is, but what it can become as object in the mind.

Absolute Reality

Windelband tells us that absolute reality is not something qualitatively other than the being we know, but the one living whole of which we can only hew out pieces to make into our world of knowledge. But this whole, if we may think it under a category, is a self-articulated organism, which cannot be spelt out from its parts.

Chapter Six: The Reality of the Concept

Basis in Reality

Reality is a universal concept. Basis in reality is an ontological premise, the being of experience.

Concrete Reality

Alone, among all other concepts, concrete reality determines the degree of potentiality inherent in the material of knowledge.

The Experience of Reality

Guzie has another of his perceptive moments when he says that when our fundamental experience of reality is abstractly refined or even directly denied for some scientific purpose, the refinement or denial would be basically unintelligible without the prior experience of that which is abstractly refined or denied.

External Reality

Being explains knowledge. (St. Thomas)

There is no knowledge of external reality without the anticipation of future experience. (Lewis)

The Knowledge of Reality

The knowledge of reality of the empirical sciences, then, consists in this: out of the endless mass of perceptions which are never entirely unifiable in the human consciousness it builds up, by means of carefully planned selection and synthetic combination, more or less comprehensive conceptual interconnexions, which are causal or teleological in structure. In this sense it possesses immanent truth in the agreement of the theory with the facts. (Windelband)

The Conceptual Model of Reality

Childe tells us the conceptual model of reality can be called a system of propositions. Truth now becomes a property of propositions. It becomes a correspondence between the meanings conveyed by propositions and the external world. Knowledge would then be a

Chapter Six: The Reality of the Concept

system of propositions which would be true in so far as they correspond with the external world. But knowledge is not a prerogative of my head or yours; only the heads of society comprehend it, and it is Society that expresses it in a system of propositions.

Is not knowledge personal in nature before it becomes societal in function?

Matter

I am in total agreement with Bergson when he speaks of matter as the view which the intellect takes of reality. Joad reacts to this definition by further defining it in this way. The intellect, Bergson contends, makes cuts across the continuous flow which is the universe, articulating it and congealing it into separate solid objects extended in space.

Bergson provides us with direction but fails to articulate the core of the problem. The direction lies in the relationship between the intellect, matter and reality. But he doesn't explain the problem. What is matter? While matter is a view of the intellect, that is, a view of reality, he doesn't tell us about the being of the view. Only when this question has been answered, will we know the substance of reality, which is matter. This becomes our working definition of matter; it is the substance of reality. Our task now is to explain our meaning and develop the theory conceptually.

The concept of matter always confronts us with the question of cause. The question is a persistent one; where do things come from? Why? How? In what form? With what substance? The answer to each of these questions will reflect the attitude of mind to cause. This is why we say, we cannot define matter without first defining its relationship to cause.

To say, however, that matter is the substance of reality, is in one sense saying no more than what is suggested by Bergson. It doesn't tell us what we need to know; matter must possess cause because it is an existent.

Cause and Matter

Matter is being; it is the substance of existence and reality; it is the nature of the real. As being, it possesses potentiality; because of its potentiality, as potentiality, it arises from cause. Cause is the source from which all existence evolves.

To be more specific, let us say that all existents evolve by means of their potential. Matter exists; it is the substance of reality; because it is reality, it is a part of the universe. Matter, then, is the substance of the universe, not absolute, but as a creative potential evolving from the absolute which is cause. In its creative potential, matter reflects the intent of cause in the universe. Intent presupposes the existence of substance with potentiality. Cause intends by means of universal substance; the presupposition is one of the reality of matter; or, as Bruno tells us, matter is the constitutive principle of reality.

There is an energy inherent in cause. This energy actualizes itself in its intellectual process of intention. This energy may be likened to Bruno's constitutive principle. Actually, it is the force with which cause develops the potential of its evolving substance.

Matter is realizable by means of the causal force which first brought it into being. Its meaning and significance is actualized by the mind as it determines its potentiality as universal substance.

For something to exist, it must possess essence or substance. This is matter; matter is the actualization of an existent. Following Bruno's thought, it is the principle of existence. Thus, matter is more than its potentiality.

Our Knowledge of Matter

It is now enough, however, to answer the question, what is matter? It is just as important to find an answer to the question, how do we know matter?

Chapter Six: The Reality of the Concept

Matter is revelatory in nature. It tells us a great deal about itself. It is not a question of matter anthropomorphizing itself, or the mind anthropomorphizing matter. It is simply the ability of the mind to realize what form and substance is saying to it. It is a limited revelation, confined to externals only, but it does project directives for intensive experimentation and analysis. Matter says to the mind: here I am; these are my externals; now probe to determine my substance. It is a question of moving from the known, through the inferential, to the unknown. It is the mind which must supply the methodology for the analysis. The mind accepts what information matter gives it; it is this information which serves as the working hypothesis in analysis. Here we disagree with Watkin. He says that the deficiency of matter in the embodied form of the knower, and in the embodied forms of the object known, renders all our knowledge partial, all our truth inadequate and incomplete. It is not a question of the deficiency of matter as it is a deficiency of knowledge of matter and the apprehension of the levels of truth which makes both matter and truth incomplete in the mind.

Knowledge is dependent on the conditions of matter. The mind, to know, must experience those conditions which is a matter of objectifying perceptual data. This is what we mean by the term evidential certitude. Evidential certitude is the act of internalizing data by experiencing the meaning of its form and substance. Burckhardt speaks of this power in terms of the creative power of the arts. It is a matter of making manifest what is within, to be able to portray it so that it is an inner thing fully revealed. The same can be said of the process of knowing matter, and what must happen if the mind is to fully understand the nature of the directives being revealed by matter.

Matter exists and so do the empirical connectives between the facts of its substance. To realize the power inherent in these connectives, and actualize the whole by means of these connectives, is to reason through an existent to find its meaning.

Chapter Six: The Reality of the Concept

The Actual

Our working hypothesis is this one: reality is finite; there is a first cause. Whatever is finite has cause.

While it is not our intention to discuss Aristotle's distinction between the actual and the potential, the thought of distinction provides us with a clue by means of which it is possible to define actuality. The distinction which interests us, but which is discussed in detail elsewhere, is that between appearance and reality. However, we now ask, what is the thought process which permits us to make this distinction?

Among all of the philosophically oriented epistemologists, it is Whitehead who alone deals with this question in each of his published works. For instance, in his *Modes of Thought,* he says that all

> actuality involves the realization of form derived from factual data. It is both a composition of qualities, and it is also a form of composition. The form of composition dictates how those forms as thus realized in the data... thus achieving new actuality with its own exemplifications and discards. There is a form of process dealing with a complex form of data and issuing into a novel completion of actuality. But no actuality is a static fact. The historic character of the universe belongs to its essence. The completed fact is only to be understood as taking its place among the active data forming the future.

With this mode of thinking before us, it is in place to define the actual. In doing so, however, we make a distinction between the actual and actuality.

What is actual is real, even though it is independent of the mind. For the mind to know something, the something must exist outside of the mind before the mind brings it within itself. There is a reality then, independent of the mind. Actuality is the potentiality of the actual, the real known by the mind because it portends meaning. There is a reality, then, which actualizes the potential and makes reality real. This is true when we say that to be real is to be experienced by mind.

CHAPTER SEVEN
THE INTELLECT AS PROCESS

Process

Scheffler quotes Dewey as saying that the process is one of trying and undergoing — trying an idea in practice, and learning from the consequences undergone as a result of such trial.

If this is a true definition of process as process, it doesn't say much for the mind and its powers.

Whitehead is much more astute in his definition of process. His definition becomes our working definition as we work our way through the problems related to process and its implicative values. Process, he says, is the growth and attainment of a final end. The progressive definition of the final end is the efficacious condition for its attainment. The determinate unity of an actual entity is bound together by the final causation towards an ideal progressively defined by its progressive relation to the determinations and indeterminations of the datum. The ideal, itself felt, defines what "self" shall arise from the datum; and the ideal is also an element in the self which thus arises.

This definition is not an easy one to understand. What he is saying is this. The teleological component of process is a significant one. End can be defined only in relation to means. Ends are never ends in themselves; rather, they are means to that which lies beyond. Finality is nothing more than the conditions which make it possible for means to function. Inherent within conditions is the potentiality for growth and development. To define is to uncover this potentiality; attainment is the actualization of conditions by means of the realization of their potential. In this sense, causality is a finality; it is the source of that which is latent in a condition. Conditions remain as determinants until actualized by the mind and projected as ideals now structured by the process of intellection. The ideal is a construct of the mind, achieved through the conceptualization of the datum, and personalized by need — the determination of end.

Here, without doubt, Whitehead gives us one of the most sophisticated definitions of process found in any theory of knowledge. From his theory we may draw a number of conclusions.

First. There is a dependency need which exists between process and the knower. Meaning cannot become an existent unless this relationship is operant. To know the self is to know the process whereby one fulfills the potential of the self, and finds meaning through growth.

Second. To experience is to experience the meaningfulness of the reality potential evolving from causal conditions. Experience is a process, and this process begins with the working hypothesis. To learn is to experience experience, that it, to be conscious of meaning.

Third. Process is the becoming of experience; it is intellective in nature, and its purpose is to determine potentiality in each existent. Process is a creative activity, moving from potentiality to actuality, that which serves as means and evolved from cause. Process is a requisite for knowing.

Fourth. Process is the means whereby the mind structures thought. It is a matter of systematizing and synthesizing ideas. In its organizational function, it determines the relationship between facts, as well as the principles which underlie these relationships.

The Analytic Process

"The analytic process itself is flexible and always subject to the data under consideration" (Guzie).

The Creative Process

The creative process is evolutionary in nature, self-sufficient, and opens the content and material of matter for inspection and discovery by the mind.

Chapter Seven: The Intellect as Process

The Historico-Social Process

Process is both historically and socially based; the historicity of process points out its working relationship to cause; the social implications of process reveal the relationships encountered by mind in determining its dependency needs. In both of these instances, form and function operate only under specific conditions; conditions are historically oriented, and may be socially determined. It is the responsibility of process to react to, and, if necessary, change the historical and social determinants. Process possesses the ability inherent in its perspective, to transcend its determinants and chart a new course of analysis in its methodology.

The Ideational Process

Hume is the epistemologist who confronts us with the implications of the ideational process and its relationship to the learning of process. Association is a key concept in this formula. What happens as process when one idea is associated with another? His answer is that one idea is transferred to another via belief. In other words, belief is transferred from one idea to another by means of association.

The question we raise at this junction pertains to the pivotal concept of association.

What takes place as movement in the process of analyzing ideas as ideas?

What directives are inherent in association to assure the movement he calls transfer?

We contend that ideas learn from ideas; here is the true ideational process. We are dealing with the implications of this process on every page of this study. Some of the implications the ideational process raises, and which must be answered are these: what are the objects of mental processes? Are they derived only from sensation and reflection? Is it possible to distinguish between mental processes, their contents and their objects? Is it possible to possess knowledge of the perceptual

Chapter Seven: The Intellect as Process

process by means other than reflective thought? Why does a certain reasoning process yield certain types of conclusions? In what way does process consolidate the associations of perception? All of these questions must be answered if we are to understand the meaning of the ideational process.

Power

What is Power? Questions

What is the power which enables the human mind to function? From what does it derive its existence and essence? What is the structure of power? Is power related only to the senses? If so, does this imply that the only existent power is the power of sense? What is the source of the being of power? Is it from the human understanding?

The Direction of Power. Questions.

Is it possible for the mind to direct its powers? If so, what is the nature and source of the power which directs the mind? Is the power directive inherent in the act of the mind? Or, is it the act of the mind which is the source of power? The difference here lies in the determinant of the nature of the power and its cognitive perspective.

To Know a Power. Questions.

When do we know a power? Is it only when we know the presuppositions inherent in cause? What creates the cause and therefore determines the nature of the effect? Is knowledge of power gained when we know the nature of the relationship between cause and effect? Is it cause which "produces" effect? If so, what must we know about cause to be thus conditioned? Is the power of which we speak inherent in the conditioned presuppositions of cause?

The Object of Power. Questions.

What is required to activate power? Is it the act of knowledge? Or, is it the willingness to act via the intellective process? Is it the act of the will to know? Is the will the object of power, then? What is in the essence of being which keeps from the mind the power to function? Is the object of power the thought process itself? Or, is it the being of the thought process? Is it power which enables the mind to conceptualize the idea? Perhaps it is the data which is the object of power. Is the object of power realized in what the intellective process makes of its object, therefore, what it knows? Is this not the source of cognition?

Cognitive Power

In defining power, it is necessary to posit two premises. First, the power of the mind is cognitive in nature. Second, this power is the active force which enables the mind to function according to the principles operative in the intellective process.

These premises alert us to a number of problem areas in making power cognitive in nature. The first of these might be suggested in this way. Is cognitive power realizable only in its potentiality?

Cognitive power provides the means for the mind to functionally establish a relationship with its object, and determine the necessary methodology to be used by the intellect in its analysis of the object. In this sense, cognitive power is only realizable in its potentiality; it is an enabling functionary, pre-requisite to the operation of the mind. Here is movement toward the mind's actualization of its object, permitting the mind to experience the meaningfulness of the object; this is knowledge gained by the cognitive perspective of power. Power functions by means of the acts of knowing.

Knowing Power

St. Thomas insists on strengthening the above stance by saying that our powers exist, as knowing, only in so far as the object is present. He continues. "A potency must first be brought to bear on an object before it can be directed to its own act; indeed the act of a potency must be understood before one grasps its reflection on that act."

Guzie interprets this. For every knowing power has this relation to the object which is naturally proper to it. He then quotes Aquinas as

Chapter Seven: The Intellect as Process

saying: that when it does not possess it, it tends toward it, and when it does possess it, it is at rest with it. This is Aquinas' way of describing, says Guzie, with reference to the structure of man, the basic fact of human experience that underlies all learning — "all men by nature desire to know."

Mind

To define the mind it is necessary for the mind to react to itself. The mind must answer to questions posited by itself. This is not a paradox; the mind must ask the mind what it is, and how it functions. To answer the latter, it has been suggested by a number of epistemologists that there are two sources of knowledge, sensibility and understanding. Furthermore, it is pointed out that the senses give us knowledge, and understanding forces us to think the object or knowledge. Some of these philosophers imply there might be a common bond between understanding and sensibility, perhaps this bond is the mind. It is only the mind that can give us the answer.

The question we must raise, then, to incorporate all the questions suggested above is this one, by what means does the mind know itself, and how is it able to validate its own processes? To ask the question in this way implies that the mind, in order to even exist, must be an active functionary; one might even say, it is an active functionary of its own being. A passive mind cannot exist. If this were true, the material of knowledge likewise could not exist. What exists has purpose; without the teleological dimension, mind would be meaningless to itself.

For the mind to discover itself, it must experience its own potential by means of its principles of operation. This is an analytical process; it takes place within experience, and permits the mind to transcend itself, reaching beyond itself in order to know its object. To know, the mind must penetrate its object and analyze its structure. This is the way in which the mind realizes its own potential.

The mind does not bring anything to experience; rather, it

experiences the existent. This relationship provides the content to experience. It is both content and method which provides the criteria for the value judgment underlying the ability of the mind to interpret its own potentiality. Within content is the reason for its existence. Method serves as the construct of the proposition; it is the proposition which serves as the hypothesis, postulating reason.

The mind is well aware of its responsibility to examine its objects. But this is not its first responsibility. Before it can discover potentiality in the material of knowledge, it must become fully conscious of what it is to itself. This does not imply that the material of knowledge is innate in the mind; this is not possible since the mind reacts to what is external to it, but in this process, the reaction is internalized together with its objects. This is the way the mind experiences itself as the functionary of the process of intellection. The mind uses its content to internalize the content of its object. The mind possesses a potency, then. It experiences that which confronts it, as well as that which it confronts. This is the process of conceptualization. It is a function which carries the mind far beyond what Locke said it is; the mind is not a tabula rasa, and it is not subject to experience in order to gain its content, namely, ideas. The mind cannot function in a vacuum. It functions as it experiences existents. It experiences ideas as ideas form ideas. Its being is dependent upon its content for actualization.

Mind is spiritual matter operating upon its own content. It is the process of perception uniting subject and object, experiencing the quality of a relationship. Inherent within every relationship is the problem of correlation between cause and effect.

The Relationship Between Cause and Effect

Effect is not an automatic reaction to an impersonal cause. There is a teleologically-oriented particular present in cause. Cause is purposive, therefore positive, in nature. It is within its purpose that its potentiality lies. Cause possesses the power to generate a number of effects, each of which is subject to interpretation and validation by the mind. Cause is

Chapter Seven: The Intellect as Process

an object which must be internalized in order for the mind to know it. In the process of intellection, the mind assumes the rule of cause so that it can more effectively control effects. To conceptualize an effect is to determine the potentiality of its cause and actualize its conjunctive principles. In this sense, effect is inherent within cause; it is cause which brings effect into being. Since cause is assumed by the mind, the operational factors are personal and purposive. A word of caution is in order. This does not say that whatever the mind conceives becomes effect. Rather, it is what the mind conceives of as cause, and in cause, its determinants, that become effects.

How is this done? The mind relies on ideas in order to function; its capability depends upon its aptitude for associating ideas in order to determine their potentiality. Inconsistencies and contradictions are eradicated, and the principles underlying relationships are applied in larger contexts. All of this, of course, carries many implications. The first implication is this. The essence of the mind is more than its substance, and it functions through its perceptions structured by the thought process. Thus, perception is not synonymous with the mind; rather, it is a functionary of the mind. Secondly, the mind is not a receptacle which serves as a container for perceptions. It is the mind which perceives and provides both method and content for the validity of the perception.

Descartes enjoys confronting us at this point in our discussion. He would criticize us for not making the proper distinction between mind and matter. You will recall that he believes matter to be extended substance and mind thinking substance.

The question we raise evolves from a statement made above. The essence of the mind is more than its substance. It is this position which would upset Descartes. If mind is substance, albeit extended substance, how can it itself, since to know, it must react to what confronts it? Here is the problem which must be resolved in the relationship between cause and effect.

Chapter Seven: The Intellect as Process

Mind and Reality

Because it is an existent, the mind is real. Moreover, it is the mind which determines what it means to be real. Reality is more than the content of the material of knowledge; it is more than an object in time and space. It is more than a thing which can be touched or its presence sensed.

Mind evolves when its ideas experience the qualities of their content. This is quite different from Lewis' position. For him, the mind "constitutes conceptual interpretations such as geometries of different kinds, which are *a priori* because they are brought to experience" (Farber).

Lewis, like so many others, finds it quite impossible to believe that nothing is brought to experience. The mind experiences what is. As it experiences, it finds meaning. This is the learning process. For the mind to know, it must first know itself. It literally experiences itself. This is the structure of the thought process. It possesses its own perspective; this perspective evolves from mind as cause and the value conditions suggestive of its purposes.

The epistemologist Maritain is very conscious of this problem, and gives it a prominent place in his theory of knowledge. He reminds us that the mind is not satisfied when it merely attains a thing, that is, any datum whatever, but only when it grasps that upon which that datum is founded in being and intelligibility.

Maritain brings to the front two further questions, both of which will be considered at a later point in this book, namely, explanatory knowledge, and knowledge by demonstration. Both of these questions are likewise concerned with a mutual problem. What has reality to do with satisfying the mind? The answer is a simple one. The mind is satisfied when it experiences the real; to experience is to find meaning; meaningfulness is a quality of reality.

Qualities are ascertainable because they are empirically founded;

Chapter Seven: The Intellect as Process

qualities are qualifiers of reality, they are inseparably bound to their content. Moreover, they serve as the empirical guide to the process of intellection. Neither the subject nor the object can free itself from the properties of matter; both are the essence of existence.

The language of reality is matter; it is the symbolism of essence. The mind reacts only to essence, even the essence of spirit. Even spirit has content and structure. While the mind can conceive of spirit without matter, the conceptualization is one as with matter, i.e., essence. Knowledge is never beyond the natural order; even the infinite and absolute is abstracted and known as an integral part of the being of the sensible world. The qualities of the absolute make it possible for the absolute as cause to be known. What can be known must be known by means of that which is real. To be known, the mind must enter the absolute; as an object of knowledge, its qualities confront the mind as realities, ready to be acquired by the mind when understood.

To deny there is interaction between mind and matter would force us into the footsteps of Descartes. We are not ready to take that path as yet. This is the reason.

The mind is constantly busy at many things. Its efforts are indefatigable. It wants to know; but at the same time it wants to know it wants to make certain that what is known is true. It is interested in cause; it recognizes that in cause lie first principles. It is well aware of the fact that it must establish the criteria of truth; to do so, the mind of mind must be open to the revelatory powers of essence; that is, form and matter. It must test its own procedures and justify its own methodologies. It recognizes its need to move only when validated natural principles have been determined. All this demands deep interaction between mind and its objects.

The mind is real and its content is real. The mind cannot function without its content. Content is the essence of mind; it serves as the working tool of the mind. It is the only way in which the intellect can know itself.

Chapter Seven: The Intellect as Process

Descartes failed to see that mind and matter are not diverse substances. Here we are closer to Berkeley who looked upon the relationship as one of linking mind and ideas. If Berkeley meant that the mind is always dependent upon its ideas, he was correct. The mind is never caught short; it is always processing ideas and determining their value. The mind wants to verify everything which it possesses. Therefore, it is always at work upon its essence.

The mind concerns only the real being. Every object of thought is real in the same sense that ideas are real. For ideas to exist, the mind clothes them with qualities of essence. To strip them is to destroy what was real. As long as they are clothed, they remain beings of reason.

The Mind as Creator

It may appear as a paradox, but the mind does create, using its verified ideas, its objects. In one sense, then, the mind creates its objects of thought. It does not create the essence of the object but only the potential inherent in its qualities.

Essence, or what we prefer to call the material of knowledge, is the source of constant confrontation to the mind. The confrontation arises when the essence of the object meets the essence of the subject. The mind now must decide what it wishes to do with the object. This decision is the one which will affect its perspective of creativity. Here you will sense that we are not an adherent of Russell's neutral monism theory. His position destroys the concept of mind as creator. What makes the mind a creator is the thing Eddington had in view when he said: "We have found that where science has progressed the farthest, the mind has but regained from nature that which the mind has put into nature."

In this confrontation, the relationship between mind and the material of knowledge, is always a meaningful one. It is only in a meaningful contest that the mind is enabled to conceptualize the potential inherent in qualities. The process of conceptualization is empirically based; it is dependent upon the constructs which, in turn, are based on the ability of the mind to apprehend the degrees of truth. Meaning first resides in the object, awaiting realization by the mind. When this has been achieved, the mind is then free to exert itself even more forcibly; it requires this freedom for its creativity.

As a creative force the mind must first experience itself; this means knowing the content of its own mind. Whatever is revealed to it as essence is mental. To validate the mental is the supreme task of the mind; it is the mind validating its own content. The mind knows itself in order to know its objects. It is the use of its content which suggests to the mind its creative potential. Creativity has as its aim to discover the nature and significance of reality and permit it to reveal its applicative values. These values concern themselves primarily with the spiritual reality of the natural order.

Mind and the Thought Process

What happens when I think? What do I use when I think? What must confront me in order to instigate the thought process?

There is a world about which we think. There is a world which forces us to think because it confronts us with its objects. And yet, there are not two worlds, because it is the mind which makes them one. There is one order in reality, that which is comprehended by the mind; reality exists to reveal its potential through which the mind comprehends its own being. The mind generates only what is real. This is the meaning of the thought process. The process has as its aim the generation of movement enabling the mind to move through its relationship with what it knows to what it is able to create. The creative function of the mind is to build up its object, strengthening its structure, by using its potential for the discovery of what is yet unknown. This implies knowing the nature of its object and discovering its positivities. This is accomplished through the cognitive capacity of the mind.

The thought process is the principle of life. It is an intellectual tool, the purpose of which is to unlock the undiscovered secrets of reality. The thought process functions on the premise that the mind exerts the final authority over the relationships existing among its ideas; it has as its responsibility the need to locate effect in cause. To trace retrospectively the determinants which are found in effect and discover the projective qualities of cause, is to realize the power inherent in the thought process.

The mind is what and how it thinks; it is the quality of its own being. Therefore it cannot be other than what it thinks itself to be. This provides the locality for its responsibility. Its essence lies in the quality of its ideas. It is not possible to separate the mind and its faculties of thought. Such a stance suggests that mind could exist outside of the natural order. This would preclude the mind from participating, through its modes of thought, as the process of intellection. It is the thought process which suggests that our problem is not to determine how the mind works, but how the mind operates as an integral part of the learning process.

Mind, Intellect and Will

Mind is both will and intellect. The epistemologist who makes a distinction between mind, will and intellect destroys one of the most potent qualities of being. It is the concept of being which permits us to say that mind is both will and intellect, and yet mind is neither will nor intellect, in the same way that will is not intellect. Mind cannot be defined without alluding to will and intellect, just as will is dependent upon intellect, and intellect is meaningless without the mind. The distinctions between these concepts must be kept clear, and yet the oneness of the three must be realized in order for each to be defined.

The mind, in association with will and intellect, functions to achieve one purpose, the actualization of an object. This is staying that the mind functions with the will and intellect; mind cannot act without its components, just as it could not act if it were blank. We agree with Descartes; the mind can never be blank. In the same way, it cannot operate without will and intellect. It is the will and intellect which moves the mind to act. This is Aristotle's position; he said that only mind can be a self-moved mover.

We said earlier that it is mind which possesses authority over its ideas. The source of this authority is the intellect as motivated by the will. From the same source, effects trace their determinants to cause, and cause portends its effects.

One of the vital concerns of the intellect is the concept of perception. The reason for the concern centers in the nature and scope of perception. To perceive is to experience meaning. This is the process towards which the mind moves in intellection. To be able to perceive is one aim of the mind. But it is not the only one. Therefore, it is a bit illusory to suggest that the mind has never anything present to it but the perceptions, and cannot possibly reach any experience of their connexions with objects. (Hume)

It is the will and intellect which makes the world "mind-like," to use a thought of Hegel. Here is Hegel's idealism in all of its epistemological glory. He asked a very important question, how can our minds grasp the world?

Reality is mind-like. It is mind-like because the reasonable is real, and reality is reasonable. For Hegel, reality and reason are identical. This is what we have been saying above. Whether or not we want to follow him to the next step when he says that the mind is the world, is debatable.

Plato's position is a bit closer to our thinking at this point when he says that the mind has immediate contact with the whole plane of reality. This, we say, is the responsibility of the intellect.

The Mind and Intuition

One of the most forceful components of the intellect is intuition. While intuition is a topic which will be discussed in detail at a later point in the book, it is now sufficient to say that its responsibility to the mind is identified with its ability for conceptualization.

Intuition is that part of the intellect which makes it possible for the mind to abstract its contents. And this, of course, requires the aptitude for conceptualization. The mind intuits its own actions, that it, the implications of those actions. Implications ride upon the theory inherent in potentiality; potentiality, in order to be actualized, is dependent upon the use which has been made of concepts. This process bespeaks the activity of the mind in its dependency upon intuition. Perhaps St. Thomas was being more than descriptive when he said this process is one of intuitive abstraction.

Mind is Contextual

There is a persistency about the mind; to realize itself it must function; the whole of the mind reacts to its objects. In this way it translates its contents into the unknown of the material of knowledge; the mind at this point is transitive. Literally, it brings itself to its object. Its content, as ideas, are formed and reformed to meet the directives of the object. This is what makes the mind contextual in its operational milieu.

The mind functions as it experiences. This is done in the context of its knowns. What happens by the mind is a matter of interaction between subject and object. Its search is for meaning; the potentiality of meaning is perceived through the ideas which are created. The mind constantly raises questions of its ideas; by this method it learns how to handle new relationships. This requires observation and experimentation, it also includes discussion and reflection. In the process, the mind turns upon itself in order to validate its own activity. This is the cognitive process.

Mind will find error only in its own thought processes. Mind without its content cannot exist.

The Self

What is the self in its relationship to a theory of knowledge? Is it

Chapter Seven: The Intellect as Process

equivalent to the subject in the subject-object relationship? If we believe that it is the subject who knows, to achieve this, it must know itself as the essence of its own consciousness. The object cannot know; it is to be known. The subject can know; it must know itself before the object can be known.

The self cannot function apart from itself; it functions by means of its ability to experience. There is no other legitimate abstraction then, but to say: the self is equivalent to the experiencing mind.

Consciousness

The fact that we are aware of our consciousness (conscious of our consciousness) makes consciousness a fact. Inherent in this awareness is the ability to know. Consciousness is the possession of that knowledge which makes it possible for the mind to know itself. It is the subject alone which possesses consciousness; it is the subject which has the capacity for learning. What is known is the object; to know, the subject possesses the object as knowledge; in other words, it is conscious of what the self possesses.

Consciousness does not imply that the mind herein is acting as a receiver, responding to sensations of one type or another. This might suggest that consciousness is a passive reaction to stimuli; rather, it is the activity of the mind functioning as a participator which literally creates the situation through which consciousness operates. Consciousness is the language of the mind expressing itself at moments of confrontation. This is contrary, of course, to what Husserl would have us believe, in spite of the fact that much of what has been said above hints at Cartesian thought; there are times when Husserl is more Cartesian than Descartes. I say this because of a concern of the mind, namely, certitude. Descartes recognized that one goal of consciousness is certitude; certitude is never reached other than by means of consciousness. Here we might play with a number of phenomenological concepts, but they add nothing to our definition.

Chapter Seven: The Intellect as Process

Consciousness is the world of the mind; it incorporates memory, reacts to and acts upon, every ingredient in that world, and projects from itself those elements together which it has participated in order to bring the mind to a point of self-realization. Consciousness is the assimilation of the known.

A Description of Consciousness

As a process, cognition weaves an intricate pattern of activity. Cognition is interested in the totality of relationships constantly seeking for identification in the mind. There is the realization that every identified relationship becomes the source for future dynamic confrontations so necessary for the mind to feed upon. It is the only way the mind is able to realize its own potential.

The mind refuses to finalize, in any way, the material of knowledge. Regardless of what is known of an object, there is more to be known. Perhaps it might only be a matter of identifying new relationships. When the subject possesses the object, it is with the realization that the real task is only beginning. That is, to determine its potential by actualizing the concepts which are a part of every relationship.

The material of knowledge is much like the floating iceberg. Its true potential strength lies submerged waiting for the mind to probe its depths. What is exposed gives but an indication of its dynamism. Ends for the cognitive process always remain means; what is realized is for the purpose of yet greater realization. This is what makes the learning process productive; the mind strives to build its future based on the intentions of the known.

Man learns for the sake of learning. He develops his powers of consciousness so that he can become more conscious of the limits of finality. It is this epistemological attitude of mind which serves as the source of critical thought. Consciousness at this point is motivated by two causal factors, definition and inquiry.

Chapter Seven: The Intellect as Process

This is to say there are conditions to be considered in determining the nature of consciousness. Consciousness is existential in nature; to be conscious of something is to experience its existence and to inquire into its essence. It is to reflect upon its potential. But even more than this, it is an awareness of what it means to be conscious at the moment of confrontation between subject and object, and cognizant of what the object does and can mean for the mind as it moves in to possess the object.

Consciousness Possesses a Content

It is Professor Eddington who is quite adamant in suggesting that consciousness has content. He does not hesitate to say that the only things known are the contents of our consciousness. This position raises a number of questions, particularly related to the problem of perception. From this problem the question might be asked, is it possible to define consciousness because it is its own content? This question might cloud the issue depending upon the given definition of content. To define content as data will add to our problem. To define it as premise and fact gives us greater freedom.

There is no difference between things and knowledge. Both are candidates for possession by the mind. It is the mind which makes the two as one. In this sense they are content. In other words, I know things as the material of knowledge. This is what gives to the material of knowledge its objective content.

What is known is the content of consciousness. The mind then, is conscious of itself as the knower, and is also aware of the premises and the factual bases of its content. What comprises the content is the degree to which the mind has absorbed the implications of the relationships between facts. In this way the mind measures its material. It is a cognitive process, but designed by existential perspectives.

Consciousness is a fact; moreover, I know why it exists. I am conscious of the fact that I am conscious. Consciousness is the basic ingredient in the process of intellection.

This factor was of great importance to Aristotle. He showed a profound reverence for the data of consciousness; this attitude far transcended his concern for what he called a number of questions in his mind which were to aid him in clarifying distinctions between his position and that of his master Plato. Aristotle shed the airy feathers of idealism that had been so carefully groomed by his teacher; from now on, every one of his words were to be encased by a thick empirical coating; his position with respect to the content of consciousness was to label him a realist. As a realist, he was to place a different connotation upon the concept of experience. Idealism spoke a different experiential language. He was forcing himself to develop a new nomenclature; to define thought and consciousness now required a different set of premises. But he would cling to some of the old, for the concept of thought still required a relationship with reality, and the potentiality of the abstract was still real to him. The intellect, he knew, was the pivot of his epistemology; it is real and yet abstract because of its immateriality.

The human senses cannot be ignored; there is an objectivity about them. This is one of the ways we apprehend content; we become conscious of what is real. Consciousness is a reality and yet it is reality which transcends reality; this is not a paradox because it is the way we know reality, that is, by means of the content of consciousness.

Consciousness is Reality

Consciousness is not a reality; it is real. Consciousness is conscious of its own existence; its task is to open itself to itself.

Consciousness is the means by which the learner experiences the real with the real. And yet, the learner does not experience consciousness; consciousness is the process of experiencing itself. It is the experience of being.

Reality is not a given, just as we do not say that existence is a given. The meaning here is found in the identification of reality as being. The realms of being include the knower, the known and the unknown. All three realms are realms of reality. Consciousness makes me aware of what I know and why, at least potentially. Consciousness also makes me aware of the potentiality of the unknown. I am aware of the facts which as yet await my understanding. For me to be able to understand them means they must exist before this can take place. Reality is, whether or not I comprehend its structure and meaning. Deductively, I have leaned on premises which assure me there is no such a thing as an entity. What exists does so because of structural supports. I may not know what they are, but they exist, waiting for me to experience their presence. To experience the presence of what is, is the only legitimate definition of consciousness as the reality of being which can be proffered at this place. Consciousness is the realization of being.

Here we join company with St. Thomas. Steenberghen, in his analysis of Thomistic epistemology, describes St. Thomas as one who holds that

> human consciousness opens on a material world, existing independently of this consciousness. Through sensation, the knowing subject is in immediate contact with reality itself without any conscious intermediary. The intellect acts in close connection with sensation; the abstract concepts formed from the sensory data are authentic representations, even though not adequate, of the concrete reality, and the judgment which restores them to the real completes a knowledge of the real which is true and certain. The sense is infallible when grasping its own proper object; the intellect also is infallible when apprehending quiddities, and when it affirms the principle of non-contradiction which is the supreme law of thought.

We might have been led to believe that St. Thomas would have taken another position in these matters. He didn't, though, because he was always confronted with the question, what are the factors which constitute the content of knowledge? And, what are the conditions under which the subject experiences the object?

The mind is dependent upon consciousness; consciousness is a condition in which the mind is able to function. It is one of the conditions which permit the mind to experience meaning.

Consciousness as a Condition of Experience

Consciousness defines its being in experience. In experience, the entire process of intellection is at work. The methodology has been validated and its procedures declared operant. Relationships are being defined and principles delineated; consciousness now becomes the process of rationalization without the limitations imposed by a pure empirical demand. Such a demand would have us believe that consciousness is a datum of experience. This would force on us the belief that experience is a setting out of which consciousness evolves. While it is true that in the process of intellection, experience makes it possible for experience to experience itself, thus consciousness becomes conscious of itself in even greater measure. In order to experience, the mind must be conscious of itself as cause. This means the mind is conscious of what the self possesses, as well as something of its potentialities. Consciousness presupposes experience. Consciousness is the process of experiencing. In consciousness, the mind experiences itself.

Consciousness is Becoming

It has been stated a number of times that consciousness is a known by the mind; because its prime quality is its ability for development, it is correct to say that consciousness is becoming. It is aware of its own presence and it can experience its own potential. This it does in terms of its objects. This is the same as saying the mind is conscious of its consciousness. Descartes was saying the same thing when he said, "I think." To say I think is to be conscious of what it means to think. To

Chapter Seven: The Intellect as Process

think is the becoming in the learning process.

Consciousness is becoming because its process makes it possible for the intellect to function. But how does the mind test the validity of the techniques used in the process of intellection? How does it test its own consciousness? In its process of becoming? Hawkins has the answer. The final proof, he says, lies in the fact that our analysis of being has not been a mere manipulation of words or concepts.

Steenberghen would doubt if this is sufficient proof. He adds another dimension. Most of the elements, he says, immediately present to our consciousness are evidently contingent in the sense that they can disappear without destroying the consciousness itself.

Awareness is a developmental sort of thing. It is always in the stages of becoming. Consciousness of the self as mind may be characterized in the same way. There is a cognitive contingency present in all becoming. There is an awareness of qualities in content; meaningfulness grows; the mind apprehends by degrees. Here is consciousness in the process of becoming.

The Abstractions Which are Consciousness

It is the mind conscious of its own being that is able to deal abstractly with its objects. Abstract thought is the means used by the mind to place special emphasis upon what is being learned. It is aware of its need to emphasize specifics as it searches for grasping points on the unknown. A whole comprises parts; parts are comprised of parts; to secure a mind-hold on a specific is to place emphasis on detail. When the mind begins to unify specifics, a totality begins to emerge. What this totality might become is the aim of abstract thought.

If we wish, we might think of this process as an empirically based intuitional consciousness. It is the prerogative of intuition to apprehend the nature of reality; to do this, the mind abstracts details by working on the qualities of the existent. In this way, the details remain as details of the object, and become details in the mind; in other words, in the

Chapter Seven: The Intellect as Process

mind which intuits them. Cognition employs the abstract ability of the mind to intuit value in reality. It is the one means possessed by the mind of objectifying the content of its objects. Consciousness, then, is the conscious perception of what the qualities of an object portend as knowledge. This is exactly the epistemological stance of Aristotle. He recognized that in human consciousness there is the recognition of potencies in every object; it is these potencies which serve as the principles of the nature of reality.

Consciousness is the transcendent quality of the mind. The mind finds it impossible to get behind consciousness; it is in consciousness that the mind begins its process of intellection in its search for knowledge. In this sense, consciousness is the basis of all knowledge.

The Intellect

The Laws of the Intellect

We begin with a question, what and where is the source of law in nature? Is it not in nature itself? Does not the universal function according to its inherent regulative directives? Law evolves from cause, indeed, first principles. Law is the regulatory principle emanating from cause and expressing itself in essence, the structure of being.

What about the relationship of mind and law? Is it possible for the mind to bring regulatory principles into being? And call them laws? Are laws applicable to universals alone? Is mind a universal? If it is, is it also cause? Is it possible to impose laws upon nature? Kant seems to believe so. He says our intellect does not draw its laws from nature, but imposes its laws upon nature. Perhaps we should make a distinction between immutable laws of cause, and the principles which evolve from the mind in the process of designing theory. Or, is it possible that we observe existents in the light of theories designed for that purpose?

The Nature of the Intellect. Questions.

How does the mind, which uses the powers of the intellect in order to function, know the nature of its functionary? Does the mind impose its other functional attributes upon the intellect in order to determine its nature? Does the intellect determine its own nature? Or, is it made to conform to things, as suggested by Regis?

The Structure of the Human Intellect

Guzie tells us two things about the intellect. First, it is immaterial and possesses no sensory organ; second, it needs the imagination in order to operate. Ducasse speaks of the intellect as reason or discursive intelligence. For him, structure implies a faculty of reasoning, that is, in so far as it has the power of combining its concepts and judgments. The question we raise is this, is it the intellect which makes available to reason and consciousness the potentiality in meaning? What is the epistemological setting in which the intellect understands its object? Does the immaterial use the material such as sense powers in order to understand? This problem was of constant concern to St. Thomas. Likewise, it confronted Kant who spoke of it in his *Critique of Judgment*. Cassirer identifies this concern of Kant; Kant, he says, raises the question whether it is possible to discover a general criterion by which we may describe the fundamental structure of the intellect and distinguish this structure from all other possible modes of knowing. After a penetrating analysis, Kant is led to the conclusion that such a criterion is to be sought in the character of human knowledge, which is such that the understanding is under the necessity of making a sharp distinction between the reality and possibility of things.

It is this distinction which we are in the process of making.

The Work of the Imagination and Intellect

It was suggested above that the intellect works closely with the imagination; Regis in the footsteps of St. Thomas takes us one step beyond this by saying that our intellect can do all the work of the imagination, for the object is not only present within it as principle of knowledge, but also an immanent term of this same act.

Chapter Seven: The Intellect as Process

The Object of the Intellect

St. Thomas gives us the delineation we are after. The object of the intellect, he says, is the true whereas the object of the will is the good. Now there is a certain kind of truth which excludes even the appearance of falsity, as may be seen in the evidence of first principles which the intellect cannot escape without by the fact assenting to them. St. Thomas continues. There is also a kind of falsity which excludes every appearance of truth, and to which the intellect can in no way assent.

The Nature of the Intellect's Operation

While we adhere to a proposition cited above, the intellect is an immaterial power of the human mind, the nature of its operation is determined by the cognitive perspective of the mind in conjunction with its physical components. This is to say, there is a dependency upon matter and its generative and reactive powers.

This is the epistemological stage or setting of which I spoke earlier, and which prepares us for the implications of St. Thomas' words:

> The intellect has two operations. One, called the apprehension of indivisibles, by which we know the quiddity of everything; the other which composes and divides by forming an affirmative or negative enunciation. To these two operations correspond the two real aspects of things. The first operation has to do with the nature of the thing itself; by means of it the known is situated at a certain degree of being, whether it be a complete or whole thing, or an incomplete thing like a part or accident. The second operation deals with the very being of the thing, which results or coincides with the simplicity of nature in spiritual substances.

The Sensory Processes and the Intellect

How do we come to possess a knowledge of the essence of things? Is it from external appearances? Is essence of things the object of the intellect? Does this literally require objects to be external forms? While these are questions which are highly suggestive in intent, is it our suggestion to imply that the intellect is dependent upon the senses? Would we agree with Leibniz that there is nothing in the intellect which was not previously in sense except intellect itself?

We encourage Maritain to speak for us because he reflects Thomistic thinking. St. Thomas never regarded the human intellect as in itself limited to a knowledge of the sensible, to which there would be added as an illusory prolongation, a metaphorical knowledge of invisible and spiritual things.

Maritain continues. Thomists recognize, he says, in the intellect an active light (the "agent" or acting intellect) which, using sensible representations and setting free the intelligibility they contain in potency (and this is possible only by leaving aside individuating characteristics vested in the sensible as such), specifies the intellect with the help of a species impressa, a "presentative form" abstracted from the sensible and "received" by it.

What is this "agent" of which Thomas and Maritain speak?

The Agent Intellect

Guzie gives us our most reliable interpretation. The agent intellect, he says, is not what we normally refer to in talking about "intellect." It is not a knowing power; various facts drawn from experience lead us to recognize the existence of an agent intellect; this enables us to establish only that it is the immaterial efficient cause of the immaterial knowledge had by the cognitive intellect (often called the "possible intellect"). The agent intellect is the thing which "draws meaning" or "disengaged intelligibility" or abstracts intelligible species from "phantasm." However, as Aquinas remarks, the real effect of the agent intellect is the production of the formal principle or intelligible species by which the cognitive intellect actually understands what the phantasms represent: "not that one and the same form previously in

Chapter Seven: The Intellect as Process

phantasms is subsequently in the possible intellect, like a body takes from one place and transferred to another." The distinction between agent and possible intellect is made only on the analytic basis of differences in function and in formal object. The object of the agent intellect, in this frame of reference, is that which is potentially intelligible, while the object of the cognitive intellect is that which is actually intelligible. The two powers do not operate separately, any more than do the other cognitive powers that contribute to the experienced unity of knowledge activity.

What is "possible intellect" which has been referred to?

The Possible Intellect

We proceed with our discussion based on two premises:

The possible intellect possesses the power to reflect; it becomes aware of the simultaneously objective and subjective principle of its act, *i.e.,* the existence within itself of the intelligible species, and by the latter, of its own nature as a spiritual power distinct from the soul. (Regis)

The possible intellect is capable of receiving all the intelligibility of the universe and of knowing it. (Regis)

With the power to reflect, the possible intellect is the means of the mind whereby the process of intellection takes the intellect beyond itself and develops the power of its intellective potential. This does not say that the intellect does not function from its working base; it recognizes its own powers, and what it does is in accordance with those powers. It is the possible intellect which sees its own immaterial being actualized in the form of physical reality. It is the possible intellect which serves as the efficient cause of the intellective process.

The Intellect and Matter

The intellect sees its own immaterial being actualized in the form of physical matter. This proposition implies two things: first, the intellect

Chapter Seven: The Intellect as Process

is an active force and power; second, it transcends matter. Steenberghen, in his discussion of cosmic realism, tells us that the intellect reacts to matter, seizes it and affirms it as a value in itself by the help of concepts and judgments. Only a transcendent and active force could do these things.

> The intellect thus prescinds from individual existence in knowing an object. To say this is only to refine the above description of an idea's lack of successive parts and extension, for these are the conditions of individuality. The intellect's determination-to-act does not carry material particularity in the formal presentation of the object so known to the power of intellect. And since the act of intellection does not in itself include matter, the power of intellection is strictly immaterial. (Guzie)

The Intentional Role of the Concept and the Intellect

By its very nature, the process of conceptualization is intentional. What it does is by way of intent. Not only is this the way it works, but it is the pivot of its responsibility as well. When the mind conceptualizes, it moves from the working base of conceptualization which is the intellect. This means the intellect must be in control of the process at all times, as well as serving as the mind for the development of intention. Intention is a perspective of potentiality; its derivation as source are the assumptions and presuppositions of the intellective process. In every cause there is the sufficient reason for the discovery of its inherent potentialities. The intent of the conceptualization process, under the control and direction of the intellect, is to develop potentiality. It is a process of experiencing the potentiality of existence by means of a systematic analysis of its being. What the mind is searching for is conceptual knowledge.

What the Intellect Knows in Abstraction

By its very nature, the intellect is a transcendent mode of thought,

Chapter Seven: The Intellect as Process

far superior to matter. What makes it superior to matter is the ability of the intellect to know abstractly what it knows as object, the essence of reality. What it knows abstractly is the *what* the real is capable of producing beyond its known existence.

The Intellect Knows What is Causally Possible

Even though it is believed that the mind is often able to comprehend the essence of things intuitively (even to the point of touching cause), it is the intellect which makes it possible for the mind to intuit. The intellect proceeds analytically, from cause to effect, and effect to cause. This is the process which makes it possible for the mind to understand; it is the ability of the intellect to actualize the intelligibility of an existent. The intellect believes that what exists has potential meaning as well as the power to transcend itself as an object in the human mind. Here is the causal source of actual and potential meaning; to experience meaning is to actualize the object in its process of transcending itself; that is, in unfolding its potentiality. Total meaning is realizable only in determining total potentiality. Meaning is experienced only when the intellect discovers causal principles (the realization that cause exists) and their effects.

The Intellect and First Principles

It is the intellect which shows prime concern for essence. It realizes that its first responsibility is the analysis of essence; however, this it cannot do until it has handled the problem of first principles. To carry out its task, the intellect must be certain of the intent of first principles. This implies, of course, that the mind is capable of certitude.

St. Thomas gives us the rationale for this stand when he tells us that the intellect is always right as regards first principles, since it is not deceived about the essence of a thing. For self-known principles are known as soon as the terms are understood, from the fact that the predicate is contained in the definition of the subject.

Chapter Seven: The Intellect as Process

The Intellect Implies Knowledge

The intellect implies knowledge. The implication carries a need to know in depth. This it accomplishes by its method of moving from its knowledge of cause to effect, and from effect to cause. This is a movement designed to emphasize the inter-relationships between cause and effect, as well as the dependency factors indicative of this relationship. This means the intellect acquires knowledge, as Guzie says, in a gradual fashion. Confronted with the meaningfulness of things through perception, man's primitive knowledge, confused and imperfect, is gradually perfected as he works his way from one aspect of a thing to another, reasoning to a better understanding of the world about him.

The intellect strives to perfect its knowledge. It is the intellect which actualizes its object and opens its potential.

When the Intellect Meets Truth

"...when the intellect meets the truth for which it is made, it grasps it; truth becomes consciously present to it."

Without question, one of the most trenchant statements in the historicity of epistemology is the one made by Regis.

> ...the intellect must... analyze the truth with which its knowledge is endowed in order to discover its value and establish a certain hierarchy among the immanent rules it possesses. This is the role of the act of assent; and it is not surprising that this perfective act of human knowledge should have a critical sense sufficiently strong to discern, among the truths it has capitalized, which ones are characterized by an absolute necessity securing them from every possibility of change and thus permitting the human mind to count on an investment so safe that no revolution or depression of the market of human truths will ever affect the value of the stock it holds. In the philosophical world the gold standard of infallible

Chapter Seven: The Intellect as Process

truth has never been abandoned, and what is more this gold standard has been identified with the primary truths measuring all truths whose stability merits the full confidence of the human mind.

Reason

There is an insistency in reason when it is recognized as a process; it is an epistemological demand; the contention is this: there must be an intellective judgment, a criteria for knowledge.

Here is a basic proposition in the theory of knowledge. And yet, it is one which causes a great deal of misunderstanding among epistemologists. A common reaction is to suggest that these criteria must be different, for instance, than appeals to intuition. We must ask, of course, this question: does the mind, which, by nature, functions intuitively, appeal to intuition? This is a strange epistemological stance. But just as strange is the suggestion of danger when the mind appeals to innate truths.

Our problem then, in defining reason will first of all center on the question, what is the nature of the criteria of knowledge? To answer this question we ask another, what is the responsibility of reason in the intellective process?

The Responsibility of Reason

Criteria are rules, standards and judgments; these are the functionaries of reason. It is by means of the rule that reason endeavors to unify concepts; in this sense concepts serve as the source from which value judgments evolve. This does not imply that reason is only a deductive process. To realize its responsibilities tells us much more about it than this. A hint of what we mean is to be found in Hume's words:

> ...the utmost effort of human reason is to reduce the principles productive of natural phenomena to a greater simplicity, and to resolve the many particular effects into a few general causes, by

Chapter Seven: The Intellect as Process

means of reasonings from analogy, experience, and observation.

We refuse to make a distinction between analogy, observation and experience. We draw analogies because we experience their implicative values; as we observe, we experience. We now insist on this position: we reason from experience. As we reason, we move as process, step preparing for, and supporting, the next step, validating each argument and position before moving on to the next. In this way, reason operates as cause.

Reason is exercising the rational powers of the mind; it is the mind operating through its own intellective potentiality evolving from cause. This is an internal process affecting not only the cognitive powers of sense, but the conditions which make it possible for the mind to conceptualize its objects, whether these are ideas, facts, or the totality of essence demonstrative of existence. But even a proposition like the foregoing may be troublesome in our thinking. It may suggest to some that there is a distinction in the reasoning process as it relates to ideas and facts. We hasten to say that no distinction like this is warranted.

When reason operates as cause, we are saying that cause is the embodiment of all presuppositions of concern to the reasoning process. The first assumption evolves from cause itself as the creator of effect; the second is the assumption that externals exist. Here reason may be thought of in terms of its dialectical potentiality, a developmental process, somewhat in keeping with the Hegelian position. To believe something is to come to the belief because the reasons for its existence have been verified by the mind. Belief, which follows upon the development of attitude, is developmental in nature.

Reason and Attitude

Reason is the embodiment of the intellective process; as such, it is the mind operating by means of its intuitive perspective and powers of empirical perception. It is that process which determines the attitude of mind toward truth.

Chapter Seven: The Intellect as Process

A characteristic of the mind is one which serves as the intellectual incentive for the reasoning process, namely, it is never satisfied with the degree of truth as knowledge which it possesses. It wants more truth by means of a deeper understanding of the potentiality of the truth it already possesses. Here is the spontaneity of an attitude so basic in the learning process. Reason works with the assumptions which make it possible for the potentiality of existence to be realized; it works with the necessity factor in existence. It is searching for implications. Reason brings attitude into being; the reasoning mind is the mind in the process of evaluation; it is the evaluative process which structures attitude. We can say, then, reason gives us our attitudes. It is reason, in the act of mediation, which serves as the source (or cause) from which attitudes evolve.

The Marks of Reason

There are twenty-two marks of reason which we suggest permit it to function as an integral part of the intellective process of the mind.

1. Reason, itself being a process, is confronted by the process of change; to meet its responsibility, reason assumes the role of ultimate judge. Dewey speaks of this when he says that the marks of reason in this milieu include necessity, universality, superiority to change, domination of the occurrence and the understanding of change.

2. Both particulars and the universal are empirical; reason works on both.

3. In order to function, reason possesses a great deal of confidence in its highly structured value system. Only in this way is it enabled to serve in its role as ultimate judge.

4. Reason evaluates (because of its nature) the conditions under which scientific knowledge becomes knowable.

5. Because reason operates as cause, it is not an end in itself; it is a method reasoned through by its own evaluation powers.

Chapter Seven: The Intellect as Process

6. Like Kant, we believe that the given is an essential component of the object.

7. The mind wills to reason; it is reason which provides direction to the other cognitive powers of the mind. This is an act of reasoning its own cognitive powers.

8. The demonstrative powers of reason are derived from external as well as internal causes.

9. Reason is speculative in nature, but tempered by the experiential values inherent in understanding.

10. Like Descartes, we believe that reason is made for truth.

11. Reason is the equivalent of law.

12. Reason reasons through its experiments designed in conformity to fixed principles.

13. Because reason is speculative in nature, this makes it possible for metaphysics to function empirically in the intellective process.

14. Reason categorizes itself as it enables the mind to experience the potentiality of being. This is achieved through the intellectual apprehension of the nature of being.

15. There is an empirical character inherent in every law of thought. Only in this way is it possible for reason to supply the foundation of truth as cause in the ultimate apprehension of first principles.

16. To reason from cause, the mind requires the freedom necessary for transcendent thought. In this way, reason becomes the creative force of the mind.

17. Existence is the object of the being of reason.

18. The intellect is the source of verification of reason.

19. Reason combines (unifies) concepts and judgments.

20. The essence of reason are patterns of thought.

Chapter Seven: The Intellect as Process

21. Reason places knowledge in the awareness of being.

22. Truth is reasoned conformity with fact; the source of truth is found in the unity of reason.

The Limits of Reason

While we are not permitting Kant to speak for us, he does set up our problem and speaks to many of the issues raised in the preceding paragraphs.

In the Preface to the second edition of the *Critique of Pure Reason,* he writes:

> When Galileo let his balls run down an inclined plane with a gravity which he had chosen himself; when Torricelli caused the air to sustain a weight which he had calculated beforehand to be equal to that of a column of water of known height; ...then a light dawned upon all natural philosophers. They learnt that our reason can understand only what it creates according to its own design: that we must compel Nature to answer our questions, rather than to cling to Nature's apron strings and allow her to guide us. For purely accidental observations, made without any plan having been thought out in advance, cannot be connected by a law — which is what reason is searching for.

Kant is taking a position here which stands in contradistinction to much of what we have been building as a theory of reason. Our differences will be seen in the questions which we must raise.

Since Kant believes that the limits of reason is synchronous with the limits of the potentiality of experience, do these limits suggest that reason functions only a posteriori? He says that reason can understand only what it creates according to its own designs; we ask, does this imply that it is not dependent upon the *a priori*? Then, of course, there is the crucial question, does reason understand? We believe the mind understands because of its reasoning powers. If reason is not capable of knowing, does it not make it possible for the mind to know?

Chapter Seven: The Intellect as Process

Knowledge is never gained by irrational or suprarational means. Even the revelatory powers of metaphysics is based on empirically structured methodology.

The limits of reason are determined by the mind's inability to apprehend the full potentiality of cause and its effects.

Intellection

There is a premise which must be taken into account as we work our way toward an analysis of intellection. It has to do with ideas. Ideas, as Plato reminds us, have distinctive qualities. Moreover, they possess the power to transcend sensory perception. With this, we agree. Where we disagree with Plato is with his insistence that ideas are independent of experience. If this is true, how is it possible for the idea to express (directly or indirectly) an "objective or lived experience"? Is it because they have their own "subsistence"?

How do we know an idea? Is it not by experiencing it? Is it not the idea which opens the mind to the world of reality? Is it not the process of analyzing the implicative values inherent in the idea which provides a direction for the intellect to pursue? Is not the intellect dependent upon its composite of knowledge in order to function via its experience? Does it not use this composite in the structuring of its modes of abstraction? The mind is unable to abstract until it has learned how to use ideas.

We are suggesting that intellection is an activity of the mind, the functionary of the intellect, the mode of operation being purely conceptual in nature. Its role is to develop and synthesize the initial knowledge of the real begun on the level of experience.

Human intellection, Steenberghen continues,

> ...grafted upon a basic activity which is intuitive in character. This is the conscious perception which involves at the same time an intuition or experience of the non-self and the self, the apprehension of the one and the other as real. In a pure spirit on

Chapter Seven: The Intellect as Process

the other hand, intellection is necessarily intuitive because it has to perform in an eminent way the two tasks that perception and conception share in us, namely, the intuition of the concrete reality and synthetic or universal knowledge by abstract concepts.

Steenberghen criticizes a commonly accepted definition of intellection which contrasts it with sensation. In this instance, he says, sensation is taken to be a purely corporeal activity. Intellection here is defined in terms of its formal object, being, while the object of sensation is said to be the phenomenon or appearance. This way of presenting the case does not conform well, says Steenberghen, to the actual data of consciousness.

For in myself sensation is already an experience of the real, an intuition of being. It is my complete human knowledge which should be defined as a capacity for being, as a power of apprehending being as such and of recognizing the value of existence in any given datum of experience. Intellection is distinguished by the abstract nature of its contents.

Reflection

St. Thomas depicts schematically the concept of reflection. Reflection, he says, is required if the learner is to realize that the truth exists as well as perceives its implicative value. Here are the steps he visualized as basic to his theory. (1) The intellect comes to know its object. Here is the beginning of process. There are two existents, intellect and object. It knows its object when (2) the process of conceptualization confronts the intellect with the potential qualities inherent in the object. This is achieved by the intellect as it reflects upon the concepts evolving from these qualities. (3) It is these concepts which now become the objects of knowledge.

It is reflection which makes us realize that it is possible to know. To know implies there is evidence to back the statement; evidence is based

Chapter Seven: The Intellect as Process

on condition. "I know because..." This implies the possession of knowledge which makes it possible to know; this is vastly different from believing that I know. To know is dependent upon that material of knowledge which makes it possible to know.

Reflection and its process is the means whereby the mind becomes aware of its own activity. To be fully conscious of all operants at work in the mind, the mind itself must be cognizant of those factors which make it possible for it to function. The mind functions by means of ideas; the mind reflects on ideas through the medium of ideas. An idea is operational in nature; the mind is interested in its potentiality; it is this dimension which changes the idea and makes of it a concept. This process of change is the process of reflection.

To reflect suggests the recognition that every idea contains many possibilities for development and expansion; every idea is full of inferences. To multiply inferences is to generate concepts. To cross-fertilize ideas, the mind reflects upon the implicative values in every nascent concept and thereby determines, when relationships have been established, their potential for further application.

Whatever is known, is known by means of inference. It is a basic functionary of the process of intellection. Impressions are imprinted on the mind because of the inferential value of the object. This, of course, destroys the position that reflection merely reproduces an existent as idea without developing it into a concept. Reflection is the process of reason, the methodology basic to human thought.

Reflection is the means whereby the mind, in its relationship to external reality, is enabled to penetrate and analyze cause in being. What exists confronts the mind and remains as question until its essence is known. This can be accomplished only by reflective thought; its purpose is not to modify existence, but to understand it as essence. Reflection is a protective measure, assisting the mind to guard against error of analysis and judgment, the most dangerous inaccuracy being the failure to make the distinction between belief and knowledge.

Chapter Seven: The Intellect as Process

Testing the Thought Process

Confronting the mind at every step in methodology is the problem of experimentation. Experimentation is a questioning process; it concerns itself with change, certitude, quest, assumptions and hypotheses, all of which serve to open the mind to greater potentialities, as well as deepen the mind in order to function at the level of cause. Growth of knowledge comes with experimentation; reflection is experimentally designed in order to broaden the base of methodology and undergird its function as the means of validating judgment. To reflect is to experience the potentiality of essence.

To conceive is to have reflected on the qualities of the material of knowledge; to conceive distinctive qualities is to have put to test the validation process of reflective thought. In this sense, reflection, as a process, is a condition of knowing.

Reflection permits the mind to participate in the being of the object of the learning process. Its concern is evidenced in its function as an integral part of the act of judgment and in the relationship which is established between the mind and what is real. To know, reality must be understood; it is the responsibility of the reflective mind and its processes to achieve this.

The Power of Reflection

Reflection is an instrument of thought; its power as an instrument resides in its epistemological ability for analysis. As a tool of thought, its responsibility is recognized in the design of its intentionality. In the process of analysis, this instrument is used to accomplish one purpose, namely, to determine cause in being. Reflection is a matter of analyzing the implications of responsibility, and doing so retrospectively. Responsibility is inherent in cause; to determine the nature of responsibility, the mind is dependent upon its reflective abilities. The nature and validity of human knowledge finds its being in cause as expressed through the responsibility assumed for the development of the human mind. All this means that present in the mind is a recognition that cause is equivalent to antecedent reality. Inherent within every existent, as reality, is cause and purpose. Cause and purpose express themselves in terms of their nature and responsibility, both of which provide the motivation for the learning process. Depth in thinking stops at cause and purpose and their applicative values. The moment the mind concerns itself with cause and purpose, reflection, as a learning process takes over. Reflection then becomes a natural function of the mind. In essence, it is a moral function because it is a moral reflection upon responsibility. In the thought of Dewey, it is the experimental way of thinking.

Reflecting on Philosophical Thought

There have been two key concepts underlying the discussion on reflection, namely, inference and the judgment which resides in responsibility. Both of these factors demand that reflective thought become creative thought. While creative thought often deals with what is called immediate or instant knowledge, its real concern is with the antecedents of immediate knowledge. It is at this point that the learning process asks these questions; when is knowledge knowledge? What must take place in and by the mind so that the mind is enabled to participate in the object of learning? How does the mind validate knowledge? What permits the mind to draw conclusions about knowledge? What is the relationship between this immediate knowledge and the paradoxical suggestion of prior knowledge? To answer questions of this type, the mind realizes that it must reflect philosophically upon the intent of cause and determine its inferences. To judge the validity of these inferences is to determine the responsibility of purpose. Reflection has as its over-all responsibility to identify subject and object and trace the dependency factors between intellect and its sources of confrontation, the data of knowledge.

Chapter Seven: The Intellect as Process

Analysis

Eight Premises

1. Epistemological Analysis

The momentum for analysis evolves from the consciousness of reality.

2. Formal Analysis

It is the mind which knows; the senses, as an integral part of the cognitive powers, and the total components of the intellective process, are the operational constructs by which the mind knows.

3. The Legitimacy of Analysis

All knowledge is revealed in words. "...sentences consist of words... therefore sentential utterances can be analyzed into series of verbal utterances" (Russell).

4. Logical Analysis

Carnap tells us that the function of logical analysis "is to analyze all knowledge, all assertions of science and of everyday life, in order to make clear the sense of each such assertion and the connection between them."

5. Metaphysical Analysis

> Metaphysical analysis... shows that the change is not in the form, but in the relation of the matter to the form it supports. The substantial form contains, in a metaphysical implication, all that the form of the organism can explicitly express in the organism's complete development, somewhat as a logical principle or mathematical formula contains its implications. When the development of the organism has sufficiently disposed its matter, these implications, subordinate forms, become explicitly manifest. (Watkins)

Chapter Seven: The Intellect as Process

6. The Method of Analysis

The method of analysis... has been... practiced from the beginning of philosophical reflection. It was already implied in the Socratic irony; it found explicit application in the works of Plato and Aristotle, and since that time it has become a classical procedure of scientific inquiry. It is the interrogative or the methodic doubt. (Steenberghen)

7. The Process of Analysis

In epistemological analysis, as stated above, the momentum for analysis evolves from the consciousness of reality. This means the starting point in analysis is the mind using its knowledge to attain knowledge. Thus,

...we know that the process of analysis goes from the complex to the simple, from what is less in being and less knowable in itself to what is greater in being and more intelligible, from the effect to the cause, from the divisible to the indivisible; whereas the process of synthesis proceeds inversely, going from the simple to the complex, from the one to the many, from cause to effect. (Regis)

...in the process of analysis, we do not always perceive the links that unite the elements, or we destroy them without being conscious of it. Our knowledge is not inevitably complete, even .when we can synthesize a chemical substance, for the processes brought into play are generally different and we are often incapable of explaining the mechanism of its formation in nature, (du Noüy)

8. Pure Analysis

Pure analysis is not a rationalism, but intellectualism, based on metaphysical intuition. Reasoning always supposes some element of experience, or other intuition, made more luminous by analysis of a prior class concept. (Weigel and Madden)

Chapter Seven: The Intellect as Process

The Meaning of Analysis

Russell recalls for us that many philosophically-oriented epistemologists have objected to analysis. They have maintained, he says, that analysis is falsification, that a whole does not really consist of parts suitably arranged, and that, if we mention any part singly, the act of isolation so alters it that it is not an organic part of the whole.

There are difficulties, then, with respect to analysis. In addition to Russell's statement we are reminded of Tarski's analysis on how to "dodge" its inconsistencies. Popper says this means the introduction of a certain amount of "artificiality" — or caution — into its use. Here, we must ask, what is artificial about using caution in any step of the intellective process?

The view that analysis falsifies the real is identified with the familiar doctrine that the real is a concrete whole. (Haldane) Here, we must ask, is there not a paradox inherent in this proposition? Its inconsistency permits us to say no more.

Admittedly, analysis does not "see everything." This would require a mind stamped infinite. It is du Noüy who leads us out of these difficulties even though he recognizes the limitations of analysis. Analysis, he says, the only practical method we possess, does not... lead us very far toward an intimate knowledge of phenomena. It often takes us away from the main problem, without our being aware of it, and places us in front of others to which it cannot be applied because of experimental difficulties or impossibilities. In such a case it is sometimes possible to infer from previous data that the harmonious sequence, which has been experimentally established up to that point, persists beyond the attained limits, by virtue of a hypothetical continuity.

Is analysis the only practical method we possess? If so, why?

Analysis is a method upon which we are unwilling to impose the following limitation:

Chapter Seven: The Intellect as Process

An object is not a "collection of parts"; it is more. It is a whole; analysis must treat the object as whole. Failure to do this necessarily results, says Ioad, in a conception of the living organism as a physico-chemical machine; for considered as an aggregation of parts this is precisely what the living organism is. Joad, in turn, reminds us that Haldane holds this belief; the distinguishing feature of the living organism is its co-ordination as a working whole.

The working whole is the epistemological body upon which analysis works. Actually, it is the starting point for epistemological theory; the object of analysis is knowledge of being. This is Steenberghen's premise when he says we must start from consciousness, knowledge, and even more precisely, affirmation, because all the real depends on the fact of knowledge. We can speak of the real only in so far as we know it; this means, there is nothing clearer in consciousness than the affirmation which expresses and completes cognition.

This knowledge of the real is a dimension of analysis which cannot be ignored.

We have said that analysis is method; but is it the only method by which we can attain a knowledge of the real? What about synthesis? Is this method in its own right? Should we label it as complementary to analysis? Regis answers these questions by telling us that analysis precedes synthesis in the order of discovery of new truths; synthesis, he says, is prior in the order of explanation, *i. e.*, not only as a teaching procedure but especially as a method of explaining the real and our knowledge of the real. (Regis)

Does this detract, then, from the power resident in analysis? Would it be possible to say that synthesis is an operational dimension of analysis, a means by which analysis functions? Whatever our answer, there are two conclusions which can be drawn; (1) knowing is never an isolated process; it is a procedural act joining many cognitive functions; and (2) without analysis, knowledge cannot be brought into being.

Chapter Seven: The Intellect as Process

Discovery

In knowing, what is revealed to the mind? Here is the essence of the problem of discovery.

As is to be expected, discovery has always been the subject of intrigue for the epistemologist. For instance, Polanyi describes the mathematician, in working his way towards discovery, shifts his confidence from intuition to computation, and back again from computation to intuition, while never releasing his hold on either of the two. When Einstein takes a definitive look at discovery it is always a search for highly universal laws. Poincare sees four stages of discovery: preparation, incubation, ultimination and verification. Popper prefers the Bergsonian taste when he says that every discovery contains an irrational element — the creative intuition of Bergson. It is to be expected that Regis believes that discovery by means of analysis is coextensive with demonstration *quia* or *a posteriori, i. e.,* it enters into every argumentation that starts from a sign and an effect in order to get back to the existence of what is signified and of the cause when the sign and effect are more known relatively to us than is the signified and the cause, whole intelligibility is greater in itself. On the other hand, Dewey believes that sometimes discovery is treated as a proof of the opposite of which it actually shows. It is viewed as evidence that the object of knowledge is already there in full-fledged being and that we just run across it; we uncover it, he says, as treasure-hunters find a chest of buried gold. That there is existence antecedent to search and discovery is of course admitted; but it is denied that as such, as other than the conclusion of the historical event of inquiry in its connection with other histories, it is already the object of knowledge.

Köhler's concern is with hypotheses. He reminds us that discoveries are usually made by those who try to test hypotheses, du Noüy holds this same line of thought, but expands it considerably by saying that an intellectual effort does not necessarily intervene in a discovery. It can be the result of chance and simply requires the

Chapter Seven: The Intellect as Process

presence of what Pasteur called "a prepared mind," *i.e.,* a mind that can be astonished even by the most simple fact. A discovery, he says, is never looked for. One "stumbles on it." But in general, one only stumbles on a discovery when studying something else; a discovery constitutes a surprise. He tells us, though, that while there is a difference between a discovery and convention, it is difficult to establish. When a discovery is made by chance it becomes a good and the spirit of invention is automatically unleased in the brain of the searcher. From then on it functions alone, and other discoveries that are children of the hypothesis and of experimentation, often follow.

What, then, is genuine discovery? Dewey has the answer. Every discovery creates a transformation of both the meanings and the existences of nature.

Is there an order in this transformation?

The Order of Discovery

There is. And it all centers in the starting point, the point at which consciousness becomes conscious of its own potential for reasoning. The mind, in order to function, must be aware of what it has to use via the cognitive act. In other words, to what degree has the material of knowledge been actualized, therefore, ready for use by the mind? What is evident in the mind, and therefore to the mind is what reason depends upon for its power to act by means of the determinant principles which provide the cognitive direction the intellective process is to take. It is this intellectual process which, step by step, discovers, by experiencing the meaningfulness of the object, reality as truth. This is to say, there is a process of discovery.

The Process of Discovery

What is it which brings a measure of certainty to the process of discovery? Is it not a knowledge of antecedents as well as their consequents? The process of discovery is the method used by the mind to determine the logical antecedent by means of its logical derivation.

Chapter Seven: The Intellect as Process

A fact exists because of the conditions which first brought it into being. These conditions are based on presuppositions inherent in cause. A fact exists because of the operant principles of certitude which enable the mind, by means of the intellective process, to apprehend both consequent and antecedent. A logical presupposition is implied in fact as an existent.

The Scientific Discovery

What has been said in the above paragraph makes one thing apparent: in every discovery the print of the intellective process is clearly to be seen. This is particularly true with respect to a scientific discovery. Without such an imprint, discovery of any type is impossible. In fact, it is the epistemological perspective and vision into the nature of every existent which determines the depth of experience necessary to interpret reality. Polanyi used this approach to say the same thing. Scientific discovery, he insists, reveals new knowledge, but the new vision which accompanies it is not knowledge. It is less than knowledge, for it is a guess; but it is more than knowledge, for it is a foreknowledge of things yet unknown and at present perhaps inconceivable.

Polanyi continues. Scientific discovery, which leads from one framework to its successor, bursts the bounds of disciplined thought in an intense if transient movement of heuristic vision. And while it is thus breaking out, the mind is for the moment directly experiencing its content rather than controlling it by the use of a pre-established mode of interpretation.

A scientific discovery is an epistemological find the explanation of which is resident in its essence.

Potentiality

Aristotle knew how to ask the right questions. Only in this way was he able to take the position: to make distinctions and do so by carefully defining relationships is to have determined the nature of causal

Chapter Seven: The Intellect as Process

assumptions. This proposition is seen in his approach to the question of potentiality; before moving to the question of its meaning, he asks, what is the distinction between activity and passivity? What principles determine this relationship?

Hawkins addressed himself to these questions in his analysis and study of Aristotle's position:

> ...while the actuality of a passive potentiality belongs to the subject of potentiality, the actuality of an active potentiality accrues to the thing affected by it, he admits that there are cases in which a thing may by its active potentiality affect itself as if it were other.

To leave our discussion at this point would be to betray our faith in Aristotle.

We think of a thing and of its potentialities as active when it is changing in the direction of greater development and fulfillment and as passive when the change is in the opposite direction, but in any change both the potentialities of the changing thing and the powers of the external stimuli belong to the sum of the causal antecedents. (Hawkins)

CHAPTER EIGHT
PERCEPTION AS KNOWLEDGE

Intuition

The Meaning of Intuition

I agree with Weigel and Madden. They say, "The word intuition only means the recognition of meaning." I do question, however, their use of the word *only* in the definition.

To intuit means to recognize meaning. The implications here are the things which really count with respect to the definition. For example: If intuition means the recognition of meaning, what happens in the mind after the recognition has taken place? Does recognition imply that the mind has received something by means of the intuition? The question I am raising is this. Does intuition serve as means and/or method whereby the material of knowledge can be known? If so, this should be reflected in its definition. Moreover, the epistemologist would never be satisfied in determining means or method; he is interested in the *how* of both factors. He asks the question, how is the material of knowledge known? He insists that a great deal of emphasis be placed upon explanation. Intuition, as a process, must explain its own procedure, as well as the meaningfulness of what it recognizes as meaning. Another example is the implications which are to be found in this question. Is intuitive recognition of meaning any guarantee that what has been found and recognized is truth?

These examples point out the need to ask many questions about what happens when intuition is at work, and how it operates. To define intuition is to answer these questions: If intuition receives something, who or what is the presentor? Does intuition give to itself, and therefore receives what it gives itself? What does it do with what it receives? Where does it get what it gives itself? What distinguishes the bestowal act from the receptive act? What determines the intellectual stance of intuition to serve in either capacity? Does this imply that intuition possesses a synthetic nature? Is intuition a purveyor of information? If so, to whom? Can it be other than to the mind? But this doesn't tell us how the intuitive process serves the information it purveys. This is the crucial question.

In intuition something is intuited. Now then, what is the intuitive process? Intuition is the process of bringing into being an existent by means of actualizing its meaning. The mind receives as the mind itself intuits (brings to itself) understanding. The object, in intuition, is brought into the mind through the realization of its potentiality. Meaning must be actualized before potentiality is determined. Intuition has its reasons for bringing what it does to the mind via the screening devices which are an integral part of its own intuitive procedures. Intuition works with wholes; to recognize meaning is to be involved in what is whole. Meaning is derived from wholes; this makes intuition derivative in the procedural sense.

The mind intuits what exists; intuition is seeing in the real what is real via what the real can come to mean for the mind. Intuition is the mind in the state of thought; it proceeds on the assumptions of reason and the connectives which tie together in sequence the dependency factors uniting these assumptions. Intuition bases its procedural moves on the insight gained by analyzing these connectives and what they portend for still other relationships.

The Ground of Intuition

The object of the mind is rendered intelligible when the revelatory powers of the mind and the object meet in confrontation and the derivation of the significatory particulars of the object are revealed. This is the ground of being which serves as the ground of intuition.

The Object of an Intuition

We stated our interest in the particulars of an object in our discussion above. Now we wish to carry our thought another step along the way. While the mind has its object, and intuition is interest in the particulars of the object, it must be said that intuition, as an operant of the mind, possesses the same object. The object of intuition then, is the particular of the object realizable through the conceptual powers of the intuitive process. To get at the particulars of an object, the mind, through its intuitive process, puts itself within an object in order to coincide with what is unique in it. This is Bergson's position. He calls it a kind of intellectual sympathy. And this is what we mean when we say that in intuition, the mind receives what the intuitive process conceptualizes of the object and its particulars. In this sense, intuition is the insight gained in evident truth. Intuition is always an integral part (appropriated) of the object of experience. The only time intuition may be proven incorrect is when its processes have not followed the rules of logic inherent in the nature of reality.

The Imagination of an Intuition

Spontaneity is the key to the action of the mind as it puts itself into its object. There is free movement to and into the object, and in the mind's return to the self. The process is one of searching for potentiality; when it has been determined, its meaningfulness must be realized. It is at this point that we say the mind functions through its imagination. It is the interpretative powers of the imagination which is of prime interest to the intuitive process. It is the imagination which offers suggestions of how the insight might be used by the mind in its continual search for self-actualization. Imagination is the intellective agent of the mind to deal with the potential of what it receives.

Intuition and Apprehension

Intuition has the potential of seeing in its object the relationships between particulars; one of the things it is constantly on the lookout for is differences as well as similarities. This is its ability to apprehend. Intuition is interested in wholes; it strives to bring to the mind insights which are unified and integrated; that is, wholes, the unity of which has

Chapter Eight: Perception as Knowledge

been differentiated, and differences, the natures of which have been integrated.

Intuition and Understanding

The intuitive process serves as the mediator between the mind and its object. The goal of the mediator is understanding; to know, the mind must understand; there is no knowledge without understanding. And, of course, there can be no understanding without knowledge. In the same vein, while the intuitive process is dependent upon the processes underlying understanding, understanding is dependent upon the methodologies underlying the intuitive process.

Intuition and Choice

Intuition evolves from choice. This statement is based on the discriminatory powers of the mind. Distinctions must be made as the mind functions as an intuitive process to determine the relevancy and dependency factors operant in the object.

Intuition and Reason

Professor Joad gives us a concise statement about the relationship between intuition and reason. He says:

> In the last event the distinction between intuition and reason appears to be one not of kind but of degree; all beliefs are reached by and founded upon intuition or insight; the demand that they shall be consistent no less than the perception that they are not is intuitive, and the process of harmonization which reason undertakes is effected as the result of an impulse which is again intuitive.

Intuition and Time

The mind exists and functions in time; intuition then, likewise exists and functions in time. Time is the framework of reference in which experience experiences experience; in this light, time is a condition in which the intuitive process operates; it is not an *a priori* form of intuition.

Intuition and Knowledge

Intuition defines the potentiality of the material of knowledge. To do this, it must possess a grasp of its content, understand its nature and purpose, and recognize the validity of the premises which underlie its cause. Intuition relates cause and its premises to effect and its potentiality. Here is a picture of the function of inference and what happens by means of inference as used by the intuitive process in determining a method for knowing.

Intuition and Demonstration

One fact is contingent upon another fact for meaning and relevancy. The discovery of truth is dependent upon the ability of the mind to apprehend the causal relations existing between and among its material. Intuition and its functionary inference determines the connectives in the order experienced.

Intuition and Continuity

"We must not underestimate intuition, which imposes the idea of continuity upon us, for its roots are probably deeper than those of logic. The foundations of our science rest on this faith in continuity." These words suggest one vital concern of the epistemologist du Noüy.

Intuition and Being

Being is known by its attributes. It is intuition which identifies the characteristics of the attributes and relates them to correspondents in the human mind.

Intuition and Creativity

Intuition, by its very nature, is creative. It is a part of its purpose and intent to be creative. The creative urge of the intuitive process takes its object on appearance, but insists on penetrating the shell of appearance in order to find the reality dimensions characteristic of its true content. Creative intuition is the vision of the creative potential

Chapter Eight: Perception as Knowledge

inherent in an object as reality. Here is the mind entering its object in order to determine its meaning and discover its relevancy in relation to a specific perspective.

Perception

The mind is always dependent upon the use of its memory bank when it perceives. And memory is always dependent upon earlier perceptions; this is a causal dependency and it suggests to us the importance of perception in the intellective process.

Perception is important for another reason. In perception alone is the mind fully conscious of its own being and potentiality. When the mind perceives, it means it has reached the pinnacle of its powers of awareness; it is the culminating point of the mind in the making.

An interesting conversation took place between Thaetetus and Socrates. Socrates asked him to define knowledge. Thaetetus defines it as perception. The reaction of Socrates is negative because he believes that perceptions are transient; true knowledge, he says, must be of something eternal. We side with Thaetetus; his statement is correct; knowledge is perception since it is only perception which enables the mind to experience truth as reality and thereby find meaning in an existent. Thaetetus would not agree with Socrates that perception is transient; observation, yes, but not perception. There is a profound difference between observation and perception. Observation depends almost wholly on the senses. Perception far transcends a dependency upon the sensate through the use of the cognitive process.

As we move towards a definition of perception it will be to our advantage to take a look at some of the assumptions underlying the process itself. In the first place, perception is an existent, and, as an existent, the percept is the resultant of the mind experiencing the relationship between the self and its object. One of the primary responsibilities of the mind is to be conscious of the relationships which give evidence of working principles inherent in the positions

Chapter Eight: Perception as Knowledge

already existing between existents. In the second place, as the mind readies itself to perceive, a part of this process entails a consciousness of those conditions which make it possible for the mind to perceive its object. It is this inferential process which prepares the mind to perceive its object. It is this inferential process which prepares the mind to move beyond the severe limitations of observation.

We are not confronted with the functional responsibility of perception. What is its function? The mind realizes that when it perceives, the object of perception is seen in terms of more than mere appearance; it is the responsibility of perception to make the distinction between appearance and reality. That is, reality as an existent and what it portends. This means that in perception we come closer in knowing what an object is, as well as what it can mean for the mind. Perception blends the past, present and future, making of the object an historical present and future; it is a comprehension of details in terms of the potentiality of the whole. It is this comprehension power of the mind which tells us that when correct methodology is inherent in the process of perception, perception can cause knowledge.

When such an assertion is made, however, it raises a number of questions. The most important one is whether or not we can make a distinction between knowing and what is known; if such a distinction can be made, is it possible to do so in the realm of the sensate? Russell insists that knowledge of a physical world comes through our sensory organs. Seemingly, it is this stand which maintains his high degree of interest in perception. The distinction, then, if one is to be made, is between what a man senses and what he perceives. The question we ask, is it possible to perceive without making use of the sensory-organs? At the same time, is it not necessary for the mind to recognize the extremely limited cognitive qualities of the sensate? Is another epistemological dimension needed here?

Whitehead says yes. His argument follows this line of reason. All sense perception is merely one outcome of the dependence of our

Chapter Eight: Perception as Knowledge

experience upon bodily functionings. Thus, if we wish to understand the relation of our personal experience to the activities of nature, the proper procedure is to examine the dependence of our personal experiences upon our personal bodies.

Whitehead puts his finger on the pulse of our problem. It is the role of experience in perception Russell doesn't particularly care for, because he feels that it suggests that the beliefs identified are true. He recommends the use of perceptive experience. We suggest this usage as a tautology. True experience is perceptive; in essence, perception makes experience. And so, we use the word experience.

While the role and responsibility of experience is discussed in detail elsewhere, our concern now is with its relationship to perception.

Perception is the only true discoverer. While the mind is fully aware of fringes of unknown reality clinging to every perception, the object is known only as it is experienced and therefore found meaningful. The object is actualized as an integral part of the being which is the existence of the mind.

As the discoverer, perception functions on previous experience; it builds its own operational determinants. These are empirically structured, but remain as categorical concepts. In other words, it functions by means of the cognitive act.

We hesitate to allow Dewey to intrude at this point, but he insists on being heard. He says that if a perception is truly cognitive it means that its active use or treatment is followed by consequences which fit appropriately into the other consequences which follow independently of its being perceived. We question whether this can be cognitively accomplished; we ask this, using the same frame of reference, while determining if what is additive, is not at the same time immediate. Dewey disagrees, as is apparent in his next statement. The difference between assertion of a perception, belief in it, and merely having it is an extrinsic difference; the belief, assertion, cognitive reference is

Chapter Eight: Perception as Knowledge

additive, never merely immediate.

Our position is that perception not only involves a dimension of intellection, but is an integral part of the intellective process. Moreover, it is the "first operation of all our intellectual faculties, and the inlet of all knowledge in our minds." load underlines and thus emphasizes the word process when he says that perception is of, or the percept has, a quality which was not present in any of the constituents involved in the process which caused the perception or percept to occur. It is only when the added dimension cited by load is recognized that we can say that "perception gives us a first approximation to the truth."

What is the relation, then, between perception and true knowledge or truth? What is true knowledge? While we define it in other contexts, our working definition is the one used by Weigel and Madden, namely, true knowledge is of that which is. Our question now becomes, what is the relation between perception and what is? We suggest the following presuppositions. First, all percepts serve as the basis of our knowledge. Second, the how of knowing a percept is the direct mode, an integral part of the intellective process. Third, the percept itself is a dimension of the substance of thought; this means perception "prefigures" all knowing. Fourth, to say that perception is a form of knowledge, as suggested earlier, is to say that it exists as fact in relation to facts. Fifth, if perception is the "inlet" of all the materials for the mind, it must first exist as a process through which the materials are to pass.

Act of Perception

We are in debt to Farber for citing Hegel after he reminds us that every act of perception has before it the open horizon of the future. "Only the present is, the before and after are not; but the concrete present is the result of the past, and it is big with the future."

Conscious Perception

Does a percept exist which is not conscious?

It is Whitehead who uses the term conscious perception; he defines

Chapter Eight: Perception as Knowledge

it as the feeling of what is relevant to immediate fact in contrast with its potential irrelevance.

Regardless of the way he defines it, the problem still exists; it is the conscious mind which does the perceiving; without this consciousness perception, even as a process, cannot exist.

In Consequence of Perception

Russell gives us an insight into another dimension of perception which must be noted for its over-all importance. It has to do with what he calls in consequence of perception. He explains it in this way. You know that a certain proposition is false. In a word: it is possible, in a certain sense, to notice what is not there as well as what is there.

Judgments of Perception

Is it possible to say that judgments of perception are something more and do something more than contain what is most certain in our knowledge, as Russell would have us think? The reason we raise the question is this. Russell confronts us with the possibility that instead of a general principle of causal inference, to substitute a number of basic existence-propositions, each as immediate as perceptive propositions. From these, causation would be derived inductively. Now, of course, this is the stand we would expect him to take. But, he must be permitted to explain his position. Every judgment of perception, he says, which contains more than one object-word expresses an analysis of a perceived complex whole; the perceived whole is, in one sense, known by being perceived, but the kind of knowledge which is opposed to error requires something more than perception.

Here we must interrupt. In the intellective process, what can become more than perception? Moreover, this is not a contradistinction to what he says earlier about judgments of perception containing what is most certain in our knowledge?

He continues. A judgment of perception which contains more than one object-word, and is expressed in a sentence which is not equivalent to several separate sentences, must contain at least one word of which the meaning is relational. There is no theoretical limit to the complexity of the object of perception or of the structure affirmed in judgments of perception which the object verifies. It is upon the complexity of the object of perception that our knowledge of both space and time depends.

All meaning is in relation to an object. In this sense, the object serves as its own referent and contains, not so complete judgment but an operational judgment, its own explanation. Here we are on surer ground than that treaded by Russell.

In perception we have a process which moves from one operational base, namely, for the mind to perceive, it is dependent upon the total being of perception (the sum of all previous perceptions) to structure its problem as something to be known. Herein are the objective values of perception realized; it is the only way in which the mind is able to actualize the true potential of its consciousness.

The Absolute

To learn is to answer the questions raised by the mind; the solution of questions is the quest of the inquiring mind. The first question asked by this mind, what is cause? needs the absolute in order to answer it. Cause is ultimate in explanation, purpose and intention.

Cause is the explanation of the absolute; the absolute is the essence of meaning and the efficiency of purpose in what exists; it is the intention inherent in every working principle.

Deduction

Meaning is in reference to an existent; since meaning is real and thus an existent, reference may also be to itself. Deduction is the process of relating meaning to meaning.

Truth is the embodiment of meaning. Truth and deduction have a mutual responsibility; the first truth, the being of being, is what existence is; the second deduction assists the mind to discover its content; both truth and deduction are concerned with understanding existence, its implications and significance. Truth reveals the nature of consistency; the same is true for deduction. To find meaning is the whole purpose of the deductive method; it is a method which is inductively based because of its dependency upon presuppositions.

Descartes was correct in insisting that the premises of deduction and its systems must be secure and self-evident as well as clear and distinct; they are based on the insight of reason. For Descartes, all sciences are deductive systems. Here is a good place to stop for a moment and ask about the differences between rationalism and empiricism. Whenever we refer to Descartes, this question lingers in our mind. As a matter of fact, he is quite insistent that we answer it.

Deductivism and Inductivism

We have said that Descartes was a deductivist. The reason for this label has been given above. His stand was that of a rationalist. In contradistinction, there were the English empiricists, from Bacon on, who "conceived the sciences as collecting observations from which generalizations are obtained by induction" (Popper).

Here are two positions, supposedly miles apart; but is there, we must ask, that much difference between the rationalist and the empiricist? The question is a valid one. And for these reasons.

There is only one process of intellection; methodologies may be different, but the process is the same. All components of that process are related and deeply inter-dependent. The process functions as a whole; each part has its responsibility. Deduction and induction are techniques of the whole; they are integral parts of the process of intellection. Both move upon the directives of their presuppositions; the only difference lies in their individual order of emphases. Deduction emphasizes generalities and evolves from these generalizations; the goal is movement toward particulars. Induction emphasizes particulars

Chapter Eight: Perception as Knowledge

and from these particularizations evolve; the goal is movement toward what is more general. The mind operates on both working premises. To separate them into independent functions is to destroy the intuitive powers of the intellect. The mind wants things kept together; only as things are kept together will truth be realized. The intellect has been chosen by the mind to do this job. In turn, the intellect carefully chooses its methodologies; each possesses an emphasis needed by the process at a particular point in its development. In fact, it is the way the mind has chosen to check on itself, and correct its own procedures. As methodologies, deduction and induction serve to check on one another. Their responsibility is to validate means and ends.

A Process of Reflection

The mind is unable to function without its methodologies. In a sense, there can be but one methodology, its parts operating through their relationships toward a common end. Methodologies provide means; ends evolve from the teleologically derived components of the means. Both require the mind to reflect upon their potentialities.

Potentialities must be analyzed; it is a work assigned to methodologies. Methodologies, in turn, must reflect upon their own potentialities as functionaries of the intellectual process.

Logic requires of methodology that its mind be literally ambidextrous. It must decide which of its manipulative energies can be used in the existing conditions. This decision is made by means of the process of reflection.

Deduction, as a methodology, scans the object's horizon until particulars are delineated. It then proceeds to reflect upon the potentiality of the particular.

Deduction is a reality operation; that is, it brings reality into being within the mind. It generates a perspective which provides for the setting in which potentiality can be realized. As an operant, it selects and uses what is needed to make the object knowable. It is concerned with observation and experimentation; it realizes that what it does must explain what it is about. To test and predict are two of its functions. The hypothesis is always awaiting a test. Conditions must be analyzed, new information validated, positivity predicted, and the logicality of laws posited. This is the setting in which deduction operates and determines its role in the learning process.

This is the critical approach of which Popper speaks so forcibly. He reminds us that the role of logical argument, of deductive logical reasoning, remains all-important for the critical approach; not because it allows us to prove our theories, or to infer them from observation statements, but because only by purely deductive reasoning is it possible for us to discover what our theories imply, and thus to criticize them effectively. Criticism, he says, is an attempt to find the weak spots in a theory, and these, as a rule, can be found only in the more remote logical consequences which can be derived from it. It is here, he continues, that purely logical reasoning plays an important part in science.

To determine what our theories imply is an important quest of deduction. What it says is that deductive reasoning does produce new knowledge. In its delineation of potentiality, it is literally opening to the mind the truth-potential. There is no logical reason why we cannot say this will become new knowledge. This process of delineation we call reflective intellection.

Induction

The Ultimate Presupposition of Induction

"The ultimate presupposition of induction is always the postulate of the uniformity of natural law, and this in the sense not only that the same causes produce the same effects but also that the same effects have the same causes." (Windelband)

The Principle of Induction

"And a principle of induction should either make it sure that the induced statement is 'probably valid' or else it should make it probable, in its turn — for the principle of induction might itself be only 'probably valid'." (Popper.)

"For the principle of induction must be a universal statement in its turn. Thus if we try to regard its truth as known from experience, then the very same problems which occasioned its introduction will arise all over again." (Popper)

The Problem of Induction

"The question whether inductive inferences are justified, or under what conditions, is known as the problem of induction." (Popper)

"The problem of induction may also be formulated as the question of how to establish the truth of universal statements which are based on experience, such as the hypotheses and theoretical systems of the empirical sciences." (Popper)

The Method of Induction

In its simplest form, the method of induction here in question appears as a discovery of natural processes, structures, or laws, through an imaginative anticipation of what they may be, and through a testing of the anticipations by subsequent experience. (Royce)

The method of induction is an extension of the method of simple observation. It is based on description, or on the observed, but it aims to include an account of the non-yet-observed. The procedure from the observed to the unobserved involves what has been called the "inductive leap." Belief in the regularity of the happenings of nature is at the basis of the prediction of future events. (Farber)

The Justification of Induction as Method

Like deduction, induction is a method of inquiry; it is a process of determining general laws and principles from the observation of

Chapter Eight: Perception as Knowledge

particular structures. Certitude of law and principle is gained when their content is identified with deductive evidence acquired from solid premises. Both deduction and induction are normal inquiry functions of the mind; the mind functions upon premises. Newman understood the implications of this functional process, and tied it together with the responsibility of perception. With the concept of inductive reasoning lingering at the intellectual edges of his mind, and with a strong desire to unify his thinking with respect to induction, premises and perception, he said that what we have here is a sort of instinctive perception of the legitimate conclusion in and through the premises.

Instinctive perception is a reflective discrimination of premises. It is this process which justifies the use of the inductive method. It is the inductive method which is able to point out the logic of truth, and make "the truth of scientific laws probable." (Russell)

Empirical data serve as the working base of the inductive process. This data confronts the mind as inferences residing in the truth of scientific laws. In this respect, induction always sets out to prove the workability of the principles underlying cause; the premise upon which induction operates is that causation is antecedently provable. This confronts us with the problem suggested in this question, is fact always resident in cause? Our answer is yes. Cause is fact. Likewise, a validated premise is fact. Probability evolves from the truth of fact. To verify fact through experience makes it possible to verify probability through experience. What is probable is theoretically probable, thus verifiable by experience. Guzie sums up this method when he says that the inductive moments of philosophical or experimental procedure give way to the stage of judgmental organization in which concrete evidences are read in the light of scientific principles.

Inductive generalizations, it would seem to follow, then, reside in probability. Here is movement from particular statements of fact to a factually experienced conclusion. It is the premise which accords potentiality upon the conclusion.

Chapter Eight: Perception as Knowledge

Whitehead quickly picked up the train of implications which this problem creates when cause is equated with fact. Cause is always universal in nature and scope, and Farber's reading of Whitehead substantiated his justification of induction. He says that Whitehead has sought to justify our belief in induction by the rational insight that any given occasion of experience involves more than itself, and exhibits universal characteristics.

This, of course, is the whole thrust of inductivism. To experience is to realize that experience is more than the experience; it is movement toward potentiality. Induction moves in the same way from observation to generalizations and on to theory. To make it complete, though, as a scientific procedure, it requires the added dimensions of experimentation and perception.

A short while back we introduced the problem of law and its certitude. We must raise the question again. There is a problem in logic here.

Induction is a scientific procedure. Science is based on law and uses it in all of its methodologies. The question is this. Is it possible to validate a law by observation and experimentation? If not, what else is required? How is this question changed if we posit the statement that law transcends experience? What are the implications for inductivism? The questions we would have to raise relative to a strict empirical methodology are readily apparent. Perhaps Born was correct when he said that induction allows us to generalize a number of observations into a general rule. If this is true, what does it do to induction as a scientific procedure?

Does a number of observations imply induction by repetition? If so, Hume would shake a negative head.

Perhaps it is too much to expect that induction should be logically justified. Hume tells us that logically isn't the right word either. He prefers demonstrative. Does he clarify the problem when he states that

Chapter Eight: Perception as Knowledge

an appeal to experience can never be inferred from observation statements, or rationally justified by them?

It is obvious that we need to add another dimension to our thought. Socrates provides it, but Aristotle develops it. I refer here to the maieutic method of criticism of Socrates. Aristotle bases his theory of induction on this methodology. Aristotle was concerned with particular evidence. How does one reason particulars, he asks? By systematization. Is this all? No. We are led, he says, to intuit general principles. To do this, we need method. It is by means of method that we intuit or perceive the essence of an existent. For Aristotle, induction was the perception of essence; to define its being is to perceive its potential. It becomes a matter of recognizing truth through its content.

The key to induction is experience; however, it is not the delimited strictually emasculated theory of experience proffered by the empiricists.

Induction, as a method of inquiry, is too important as a mode of thought to move under such severe limitations.

Act

Perhaps the question is not so much, what is act? as, where is act? Seemingly, Dewey prefers the latter enticement.

In asking the question where, it is not a matter of location on the continuum between the Aristotelian act and potency; rather, it is a question of where on the ascendency scale of values the decision is made to act and why. The mind acts when there is a reason for it to act; there is a potentiality inherent in act which Watkin says is determined by an apprehension of value. This suggests that all action "presupposes" an apprehension of value.

This position carries us beyond Dewey's contention, with which we agree in part, when he says an act is an interaction, a transaction, not isolated, self-sufficient. The initial stage of an act, he wants us to remember, and the terminating consequences which, between them, determine its meaning, may be far apart in place as well as in time. What he is asking, of course, is the question, where, then, is the act?

The answer? Not in making a distinction between acts of thinking and acts of choosing. The apprehension of value is the realization that mind, as it functions, understands, via conative implications, the ontological bases of its intellective process. Act is the culminative unification of all dimensions of being, all tenets of which serve as directives for aiding the mind in making its decisions (after actualizing its values) and reacting to the implications inherent in potentiality. Essentially, act is the process of realizing and actualizing potentiality. It does not reduce potentiality to act; rather, the mind acts to reduce potentiality to actuality. Act is the becoming of being by means of the apprehension of its value potential.

The Cognitive Act

Knowledge is attained when the knower experiences meaning; the experiencing of meaning is the cognitive act; the material of knowledge has become a part of the totality of the functioning mind. This means the object has become united with subject. All experience is cognitive in nature; quite literally it becomes the content of consciousness.

Act, as well as the cognitive act, is the resultant of the functional capabilities of the mind to develop its consciousness of value.

Action

The thinker works with ideas; since ideas learn from ideas, here is a mental activity which spells action. An idea suggests movement and direction, both of which evolve from the presuppositions which undergird the idea. Presuppositions are knowledge which serve as working hypotheses. Here, again, is the kind of action of which we speak. Basing our analysis upon these premises, then, we say that action is means; epistemological theory must never force it to become an end. Since means imply an inherent methodology, the construct of methodology demands the dependency upon directives found in movement; such directives are purposive in nature.

Action is that positivity of movement which delineates purpose and direction in the intellective process.

Activity

Cognitive Activity

Steenberghen gives us a clue as to the meaning of cognitive activity. He says cognitive activity is without any doubt the most conspicuous of all activities since it constitutes consciousness. To this statement he appends a paradoxical dimension "...and is identified with it." What he means by this we do not pretend to know. However, our basic premise is the one to which he draws our attention, namely, cognitive activity constitutes consciousness. Without this consciousness the mind would be unable to function via its activity as the essence of the intellective process.

While one of our major concerns throughout this study is consciousness, we stop for a moment to consider it in relation to cognitive activity. In asking the question, what is the source of cognitive activity? we have no choice but to answer, the relationship between mind and its cognitive powers and processes. Regis, in echo of St. Thomas, expresses it as the laws of immateriality. These laws, he says, are essential to the exercise of every vital act, and particularly to the exercise of the superior vital energy that is knowledge.

With the realization and actualization of the object by the subject — the result of cognitive activity — there is "an existing of the known in the knower."

A classic statement of cognitive activity is furnished by Regis. We would be amiss if we failed to quote it in full. He says there are

> three universal laws governing all our cognitive activities. The first is the incoercible desire for truth, a desire that haunts our soul and is expressed by our instinctive flight from ignorance

and error the moment we become aware of their presence. The second law governs the activities consequent upon this desire for truth; it organizes the steps we take in discovering knowledge, steps that are normally a continual reflective interchange between the universe we know and the universe that is, in order to reconcile the different accounts reality gives of itself when we are its guests. The third law has to do with the results of our steps toward knowledge. If these results are positive — if man succeeds in resolving the contradiction between these accounts, dissolves their differences, and discovers a new truth, a truth more complete than those preceding it — then confidence in our intellectual powers increases, its methods of research improve, and there results one of those magnificent syntheses that have nourished the human mind for centuries.

Conceptual Activity

Conceptual activity must be classified as a transcendent quality; its purpose is to transcend the structural limitations of reality and its many dimensions.

Steenberghen defines conceptual activity as that means by which it is possible for us to account for our universal abstract representations, as well as for our ability to conceive, at least in a hypothetical way, incorporeal objects.

Creative Activity

It may appear as something of a paradox to suggest that the contingency factor in all creative activity is its intentionality. Since intention is an integral part of all potentiality, and potentiality is the working base from which all creative activity evolves, the activity which is the momentum of the creative mind expresses itself in the becoming of being. This means a movement transcending a giveness until its being is fully actualized.

Chapter Eight: Perception as Knowledge

Discursive Activity

Discursive activity is the means inherent in process whereby the mind conceptualizes the intent of its judgments. Regis speaks of synthesis as a means of discursive activity. This requires, he points out, a starting point for its movement, an evidential truth from which it draws a hitherto unknown truth, not merely the successive consideration of two truths.

Mental Activity

Joad posits a weak proposition when he says that mental activity is essentially an awareness of something other than itself. This is correct only if the mind first of all is conscious of its own processes. Only in this way is it possible for it to be aware of something other than itself. Since he would also have us believe that the character and quality of the experience which results from the activity is determined by the nature of the objects upon which the mental activity is directed. To agree with this statement is to believe that the mind becomes the object of manipulation, locking in powers of evaluation and judgment. To think is to experience meaning. The mind cannot know without experiencing its object, the known object existing in the knower.

Abstraction

The power to abstract is one of the most salient functions of the mind. This is a safe assumption; now we move to a proposition which will cause a few questions to be raised.

There is the tendency among some epistemologists to suggest that in the process of abstraction it is possible to leave the level of the sensible and move up to the "level of the objects of thought." It is the implications of these suggestions that bother us. It implies that it is possible to leave the level of the sensible and move beyond it. This assumption is false; it is possible to transcend the sensible and move up to "the order of intelligible being" as Maritain calls it, but only when the sensible is made an integral part of the transcendent process. The

Chapter Eight: Perception as Knowledge

level of the sensible is never ignored by the mind; it is a part of the totality of the functioning perspective of the intellective process.

Maritain equates material existence with the level of the sensible; this is an interesting position; primarily so because of the problems it raises. Abstraction, he says, transfers us from the level of sensible and material existence to the level of the objects of thought, introduces us into the order of intelligible being, or of what things are. But at first it only attains the commonest and poorest aspects of this intelligible being.

He continues. Abstraction reveals certain intelligible aspects which really are in things. But the very essence of things, *i.e.* the notes that properly constitute their intelligible being and explain their properties, is only attained — when it is attained — at the expense of hard labour. For the discovery of that essence must always be in keeping with the imperfect manner of knowing suited to man, and only in virtue of the properties which reveal it. And, he hastens to add, in a whole vast area, that of the inductive sciences, we do not attain it and we have to contend ourselves with substitutes, manageable equivalents.

Is material existence to be equated with facts? Is it possible to abstract a fact? If not, must facts become known only by means of the sensate?

Whitehead gives us the needed insight for analyzing our problem. Much of what he says points up the problems raised by Maritain. Whitehead contends that as soon as we abstract (and we do so to separate the notions of serial forms and of individual facts involved) we necessarily introduce the notion of potentiality. By this he means the potentiality of the facts for the series and of the series for the facts. Whitehead insists that all our knowledge consists in conceiving possible adjustments of series and of individual facts to each other And this, of course is our position. It is a basic contention in our formulation of a definition of abstraction.

Chapter Eight: Perception as Knowledge

Whitehead continues his discussion. He says, in effect, that such and such facts are consistent with such and such serial forms. Here are the possibilities for individuals and possibilities for series. The mere immediate exemplification is only one aspect of our experience.

To abstract is to determine the conceptual potentiality of a fact. This definition implies that an object of thought is known by means of the sensate as well as the abstract ability of the mind to experience its meaning. It is a matter of discovering the connectives inherent in each relationship between facts. Of course the moment we concern ourselves with the underlying connective principles between facts, we are dealing with universals.

To abstract is to depend on these "series" spoken of by Whitehead. It tells us one thing: abstraction, as a process, is never an isolated function of the mind. Actually, we are willing to go as far as saying that the essence of the mind is the product of the processes of abstraction. But we do not go as far as Hume in suggesting that our starting point for this process is only "a stream of perceptions." Nor, would we agree with Berkeley that it is enough to have a divine mind with its ideas. This implies using only one half of the epistemological canvas. What would happen to matter? As the cause or source of abstraction?

The process of abstraction is the one assurance that rationality is an integral part of the "order of intelligible being." To determine the potentiality of matter (as a part of the intellect) is the reason for the mind abstracting its objects as the essence of thought.

The *a Priori*

One of the most difficult concepts we face in the theory of knowledge is the *a priori*. It is not difficult to define; the epistemological burden lies in determining its implicative values. To point this out, we face such questions as, is it possible for the *a priori* to be independent of experience? Is the *a priori* of the mind? If not, how does the mind decide what is *a priori'"*? In determining what is

Chapter Eight: Perception as Knowledge

given, is there a distinction between the given and the known? How does the mind know essence? How does the mind come to know what is prior to essence, if this is possible? These are questions which will govern our thinking in the formulation of a definition of the *a priori*.

When we speak of experience we refer to the pivotal concept in learning theory. To learn is to experience meaning. To ask the question, when do we experience? is to answer in only one way, when what we experience is meaningful. We learn when the object is meaningful. To define the *a priori* is to determine its relationship to experience and meaning. The traditional approach is to posit the proposition; the *a priori* concept is that which is not structured by the essence of experience.

There are a number of facets which upset our epistemological stance. If a concept is of the mind, and the mind functions experientially, what might be formed without abstracting from experience is an object independent of the mind. But a concept is dependent upon the mind; it evolves from the activity of the mind, and the mind conceptualizes the potentiality of the concept.

Where does this leave the *a priori* in the scheme of epistemological theory?

Before this question can be answered, we must take another look at our pivotal problem. And very justifiably Hume calls our attention to it. He presses us with this belief: reasoning *a priori* and considering merely an object or cause as it appears in the mind, independent of all observation, it never could suggest to us the notion of distinct object, such as its effect, much less show us the inseparable and inviolable connection between them.

This position raises the following questions in our mind, is the *a priori* the object which is independent of the mind? If so, what does this imply for the mode of thought suggestive in reasoning *a priori*? Can the *a priori* be an object not structured by experience, as well as an

Chapter Eight: Perception as Knowledge

analytical method of reasoning? Moreover, is it possible for something to appear to the mind and yet be independent of all observation? To observe something means there is something to observe, if only an idea. Any degree of observation tells us that entities cannot exist; what exists contain conditions for existence. The moment you have conditions, you have dependency factors, all of which imply the presence of connectives. Connectives imply relationships.

Are there distinct objects, then? Can effect be considered distinct from its cause? What function of the mind does not permit even the appearance of distinctness between subject and object, cause and effect?

To say, like Dewey, to call it *a priori* is to express a fact, is to make the *a priori* integral part of the reasoning process. Rather than being a concept (as object) it is the process of conceptualization. If this is our position, it would force us to part company with Dewey who insists that to impute the *a priori* character of the generalizing force of meanings to reason is to invert the facts.

Not at all. To make of the *a priori* a process which inverts facts is to take from it its logical function. The *a priori* is a logical function, more than it is in the formal object of the ontological faculties, as Regis reminds us in his discussion of the problem.

> The *a priori* may also be defined as the formal object of the ontological faculties and not only as a logical function, but to make this addition is completely to forsake the Kantian point of view for a realist point of view. And to identify the formal object with the faculty itself, with its first act, as if it were a hollow prefiguration of the general form of the object that will be its natural complement, is to transform into Kantian or subjective realities that which, for St. Thomas, characterizes exterior realities. Moreover, it is to transform these characteristics of the transcendental subject by giving them a window to the real, which Kant does not give them. For the

Chapter Eight: Perception as Knowledge

opening of the Kantian *a priori* to an objective world of Noumena is a glance at a world that is illusory by definition.

If we believe that the truth of the *a priori* is formal, the question, how do we experience truth? looms large.

Experience is a matter of determining meaning in and for whatever the object might be. What constitutes the mind of experience determines the degree of validation the essence of the object actualizes. This actualization is the experiential value gained when the necessary connectives between facts are determined. Here are the propositions found in every learning setting; these are the true *a priori-,* in every case the proposition is synthetic in nature; the *a priori* itself is analytic in nature.

When we discuss validation we are confronted by criteria. Criteria are determined by assumptions and presuppositions; there are conditions which underlie principles and structure; to actualize conditions we must experience them. If we should equate conditions and cause does it change the responsibility of the mind to experience? If the *a priori* exists to confront the mind, the mind is under obligation to meet the confrontation. Here is the process of confrontation which becomes the essence of experience. In this process the mind must transcend its object.

How, then, is the *a priori* knowable? This question can be asked only if we are willing to concede that while the *a priori* is analytic in nature, its operating principles are definitive in nature. Definitive principles evolve from the transcendent mind. It is this faculty which concerns itself with criteria.

To answer the question, how is the *a priori* knowable? is to recognize that it is the object which is knowable because its conditions make it possible to be known; its presuppositions become the source (cause) of learning and provide the directives necessary to understand the connectives inherent in every principle. Here is the cognitive thrust of the *a priori.* The *a priori* permits the subject to function because of what the *a priori* offers as the material of knowledge as object confronting the subject.

The mind depends upon the propositions of the *a priori* in order to devise its intellective methodologies. It is the *a priori* which provides the mind with a synthetic perspective; quite literally, it forces the mind to conceptualize the ideas projected in every confrontation. It is the true *a priori* which provides the incentive for the mind to function. It is up to the mind to determine what is logically prior to all observational experience; to do this, however, it must experience the potentiality of the object by its analysis of the conditions as presuppositions. Kant has something to say about this when he insists that these conditions are *a priori,* but, conditions which are viewed logically are prior to sensation. If this is true, what happens to the responsibility of experience?

Acquaintance

Dewey confronts us with an important relational concept in the theory of knowledge. To be acquainted with anything, he says, is to be aware of what it is like, in what sort of ways it is likely to behave. He draws a difference between acquaintance and "knowing about" or "knowing that." He says that it is not a difference between two kinds of knowledge, one immediate and the other mediate. The difference is an affair of accompaniments, contexts and modes of response. Acquaintance, then, instead of being a mode of knowledge prior to knowledge about and knowledge that, marks a later state in which the latter attain full sense and efficacy.

Analogy

Russell presents us with a strange and paradoxical epistemological problem. If his logic is not faulty it must be his definitive premises. He tells us that it is impossible to enter into the minds of others to observe the thoughts and emotions which we can only infer from their behavior. He is correct when he says we cannot enter into the minds of others; it

Chapter Eight: Perception as Knowledge

would be interesting to know what he puts into his belief about the word enter. In one sense, we do enter other minds; the mind itself can only be known by its modes of thought, and when these are expressed, other minds can enter upon the terrain of language. It is possible for me to experience your thoughts. But Russell would have us believe that the only way in which we can accept analogy is in the sense in which it goes beyond experience, as an independent premise of scientific knowledge. We question whether this is possible. He makes a distinction, of course, between analogy and induction; he is worried by his belief that an analogical inference, when it passes outside experience, cannot be verified. Our contention is this: if it does pass outside experience, it is no longer an analogical inference. Where, then, is the problem?

Our position would be in jeopardy if we agreed with Blackstone in his discussion of Mascall that there is a contingency of existence which arises from the fact that in finite beings essence and existence are really distinct. Such belief would destroy our epistemological stance with respect to experience. While not exactly reversing himself Blackstone does give us an insight into a meaningful use of analogy. This means, he says, taking some characteristic found in our experience and postulating a higher degree of that characteristic that is shown in our experience. The change we would make is this. Analogy is experiencing characteristics of our experience and postulating the potential of those characteristics.

Change

One of the problems particularly upsetting to Kant is the question, how is it possible to distinguish between the consciousness of objective change and subjective succession? Bergson has an answer. He says that we change without ceasing (because of the nature of the living process), and the state itself is nothing but change. There is no feeling, no idea, no volition which is not undergoing change at every moment; if a mental state ceased to vary, its duration would cease to flow.

Chapter Eight: Perception as Knowledge

To all of this Dewey raises his voice. Don't forget, he says, that when correlations of changes are made the goal of knowledge, the fulfillment of its aim in discovery of these correlations, is equivalent to placing in our hands an instrument of control. He continues. When one change is given, and we know with measured accuracy its connection with another change, we have the potential means of producing or averting that other event. The esthetic attitude is of necessity directed to what is already there; to what is finished, complete. The attitude of control looks to the future, to production.

While Kant, Bergson and Dewey have alerted us to a number of problem settings, the issues raised are those which can be resolved. It is more difficult to agree with Plato. His law of historical development stands in our way of conceptualizing the potentiality of change. He believes that change does not possess a positive potentiality; as a matter of fact, he is a foe of change and would like to retard it. Change is decay, he says, at least most of it. He explains the visible world of change by an invisible world of unchanging "Forms," (or substances, essences, or natures), that is, geometrical shapes or figures.

Since this theory is not acceptable, how do we describe change?

Change is to be conceived of in terms of its potentiality. Without this dimension, the attributes of change (which describe its function and operational principles) cannot exist. The potentiality of change evolves from its situational and residential object. This says that in every existent, change is immanent. Change is an inherent part of the nature of every existent. The attributes of change are means by which the mind describes the characteristic action of change.

The second dimension of change looks like this. Because the emphasis of change is on potentiality, change is a matter of evolvement, not a mechanical transaction of addition or subtraction of being, as Hawkins asks us to be on guard against. Hawkins clarifies this statement for us when he speaks of act and potency (in the true Aristotelian Mode) and relates it to our question. The concepts of act and potency, he says, arise from a consideration of a changing thing. To this he adds it is not true that anything can become anything else. Hawkins predicates this position on four assumptions: (1) Change presupposes a successive mode of existence, or time in the widest sense of the word; (2) change as a fact needs no proof, but it is unintelligible except in relation to being; (3) a formless becoming presents no object to the mind; becoming is either the coming-to-be of something or it is something becoming something else; and (4) continuous change in a conceptual construction, not an object of observation, therefore, it involves no contradiction.

Change, then, is a potentiality for attaining the becoming of being; it permits the mind to connect antecedents and consequences, as well as anticipate purpose in the analysis of cause and its first principles.

Memory

An important premise of all knowledge is memory. This does not imply, however, that memory is knowledge. While it does imply that memory is the apprehension of past occurrences, apprehension is not necessarily a guarantee that there has been the experience of meaning. Memory suggests a concern with the past in the same way time is often thought of; that is, in relation to past events. This is Bergson's position. He says that memory goes into time.

Without knowledge, memory could not exist. Without memory, knowledge could not be defined as experiencing meaning. In memory, the mind uses its content to remember; it is a means of alerting consciousness to its responsibility. Consciousness and memory are the two factors which serve as the intellective guards in the process of change and development constantly underway in the mind. Without these two functions, logic could not operate in the intellectual process. Since change is a characteristic of intellectual movement, the mind requires guards to screen those factors which will determine the reliability and validity of change to assure development. Learning is building upon experience; experience requires both consciousness and

Chapter Eight: Perception as Knowledge

memory to render itself, as a process, meaningful. As experience evolves from experience, value evolves from value; value is the objectification of experience. It is this process which makes the mind aware of antecedents. This is memory.

Knowledge is always present knowledge. The process of intellection relies, however, on memory to make knowledge what it is at the moment of actualization. Memory brings the material of knowledge to the confrontation which is the learning process; it permits the mind to retain its contents. Memory actualizes the content of the past and makes it existentially knowable; it does not reproduce the past; rather, it brings it into the present and objectifies its meaning for the existential moment. Memory is the precondition in the learning setting. The mind is wholly dependent upon memory for the working base from which all of its hypotheses evolve. Here is a factor Descartes found so difficult to accept. Perhaps the difficulty evolved from the question: is memory belief? Is it only belief? We could see Descartes raising a number of objections at this point.

Such a question, however, is not as serious as the implications of a statement by Russell who says that memory is the purest example of mirror knowledge. This is nonsense. He is correct, however, in saying that the "general, though not universal, trustworthiness of memory is an independent postulate. It is necessary to much of our knowledge, and cannot be established by inference from anything that does not assume it."

Even though we agree with Russell that memory is a premise, and by this he means that among the facts upon which scientific laws are based, some are admitted solely because they are remembered, memory has a greater responsibility than Russell seemingly is willing to give it.

Learning has one goal, namely, understanding. Understanding requires the use of an intellectual process; an integral part of that process is memory.

Chapter Eight: Perception as Knowledge

Since memory is more than recall, it causes the mind to operate on an intellectual base, drawing from the experience of antecedents the relevancies of what is applicable, and fusing these with the content of what is an upward movement, namely, apprehension. Method and meaning combine with memory to instigate the movement which is learning.

What is learned is retained by the mind; this is memory. It is the intellect which does the retaining; the intellect is the embodiment of the power of thought; it encourages memory to be more than recall. Memory uses experience so that experience can use itself. This is what is meant by putting oneself into one's own experience. Experience, in memory, uses its own datum to experience its own potentiality. This implies that the mind, through memory, is aware of the implicative values inherent the datum of experience; it understands the meaning of experience. In this way the mind uses memory to connect and fuse experience, and determine causal direction for the intellectual process. This is the internalization process which was of great concern to Bergson. For him it meant the inter-penetration of all elements in one's past life.

Because of memory, experience remains on the conscious level in the human mind. Because of memory, experience is always referential to the human mind.

Memory and the Imagination

In considering the relationship between memory and imagination, it is Hume who works himself to the front in order to express his position. Memory, he says, preserves the order of the original events, but the imagination need not. Both are images, or, as he preferred to call them, ideas. Memory, then, is a matter of having an idea. The idea is a reflection of its point of origination. Woozley interprets Hume as saying that the real distinction between memory-images and imagination lies in the fact that the former possess a vivacity which imagination does. Ayer, in quoting Hume, makes a similar distinction

Chapter Eight: Perception as Knowledge

when he says that the ideas of memory are distinguished from impressions by the fact that they are fainter, and from ideas of imagination by the fact that they are livelier.

These distinctions are drawn to call our attention to the fact that what is working here are a number of operative powers. Imagination is an integral power of the mind, and as such, a co-worker with memory.

Factual Memory

To correctly remember facts is to have a factual memory of them. But a factual memory is more than the ability for recall. Factual memory is but one dimension of the operative powers of the mind of memory. Knowledge is the working or operational base upon which memory depends. To possess knowledge is to be certain of its content. To remember content is to be aware of the potentiality of its material. This is what is meant when we say that the ground of knowledge is... There is no such thing as previous knowledge. There are grounds of knowledge which memory actualizes and projects as fact. This is factual memory.

Perceptual Memory

Malcolm is correct when he says that perceptual memory presupposes a background of remembered facts. In defining perceptual memory, Malcolm insists that imagery and personal memory are each necessary conditions. He asks, Is their conjunction a sufficient condition? He answers. It would appear so. The definition is the following: "B perceptually remembers if and only if B personally remembers, and B can form a mental image of." Malcolm comments on the definition. First, it is not a definition of remembering but only of the adverb "perceptually," as it modifies the verb "remember." Second, what is defined is the notion of a perceptual memory ability, not the notion of a perceptual memory occurrence.

If Malcolm really means what he has just said, how can he justify this statement: "I argued that all mankind could have existed without

Chapter Eight: Perception as Knowledge

perceptual memory." He has created a paradox from which there is no exit.

Personal Memory

Malcolm raises a number of questions about personal memory. Isn't the term or label a bit misguiding? In the final analysis, all memory is personal whether it is factual, perceptual or symbolic.

Symbolic Memory

At this junction in our discussion, we shall satisfy ourselves with Cassirer's definition. Symbolic memory, he says, is the process by which man not only repeats his past experience but also reconstructs this experience.

True Memory

What is lacking in incorrect memory is knowledge. Correct knowledge, rightly understood, is the working premise of true memory. True memory is using the perceptive powers of the mind to cull from its validated material of knowledge what is applicable to experience.

Remembering

In his astute study on remembering, W. von Leyden takes us to the pivot of our question when he says that what we can remember is not just any past event or fact, but a certain kind of past events or facts, namely those that form part of one's own previous experience. It is his next statement with which we disagree. He speaks of memory as "what one has personally witnessed in the past." Now, if he means by witness experience, we agree. Otherwise, his foregoing statements and this latter one are inconsistent.

The point we wish to make emphasizes the need for experience. If we believe that remembering is a way of knowing, and we do, in order to know, the mind must experience its object. Woozley is quite specific about this. He says that remembering consists on having images which preserve the order of the original, that is, the event remembered. In turn, these images are marked by a certain degree of vivacity, less than that of the original experience. While Woozley via Hume confronts us with another problem here, the original problem persists. Whether or not there are degrees of experience is not important at this point. Remembering is experiencing by means of an analysis of knowledge and its conditions. It means remembering a perception, its setting as well as its connotations. This insistence, via perception, tells us that what we remember is the perception of something.

Remembrance

While remembering is a continuous process of thought about what is remembered, remembrance is the fact that we have internalized what we remember. While remembering is an on-going process, very much a part of the present, remembrance is of the past but of a past which exists in the present because of its inherent potentialities.

Seeing

To see implies the fact that something is seen.

What does it mean to see epistemologically? What are the implications of Aristotle's statement: I can say "I have seen it" as soon as I can say "I see it"? What are the implications of Ayer's discussion of Ryle: "To look and see is not to look around and do something else, subsequently, or at the same time; it is to look successfully"?

To see something successfully is to see what it is. The *what* in epistemological theory is equivalent to knowledge. Does this imply: to see is to know? It does, if we are willing to make of seeing an intellectual process, introspective in nature, with the ability to be concerned not only with the present, but the past and future as well. Seeing is the ability to interpret, by means of the introspective process of intellection, the essence of consciousness, the reality of which is the potentiality of existence.

Chapter Eight: Perception as Knowledge

Repetition

To say that repetition is habit or custom is to give to repetition a narrow precipice on which to balance.

Hume urges us to believe that repetition is based on similarity or resemblance.

> For wherever the repetition of any particular act of operation produces a propensity to renew the same act or operation without being impelled by any reasoning or process of the understanding, we always say that this propensity is the effect of custom.

The key which opens the lock keeping us from our real problem is the directive inherent in these words: any reasoning or process of the understanding.

As Guzie reminds us: repetition does not necessarily bring about an act of understanding. That is, unless there is an intellective process which leads to an understanding of meaning.

> If there is no potential meaning represented in the sensory material that is more and more firmly ingrained in the memory-imagination through repetition, actual meaning cannot result. Thus, repetition does not of itself render a symbol communicative. If, on the other hand, the material represented in phantasms, verbal or otherwise, is at the first instance potentially meaningful, the intellect operating according to its nature will actually understand the meaning.

The Sentence

A sentence of Russell's gives us the opportunity to confront ourselves with a problem which must be analyzed.

> A sentence belongs to logic if we can be sure that it is true (or that it is false) without having to know the meanings of any of the words except those that indicate structure.

Chapter Eight: Perception as Knowledge

We ask you to read the above sentence again. Are there words in the sentence which do not indicate structure? Moreover, what can be judged logical unless what is said by means of words is logical?

There are those epistemologists who would have us believe that it is possible to make a distinction between a sentence and what it means. We question this proposition. A sentence comprises words, and behind words are ideas. Whether the words are placed in correct linguistic order is not our problem at the moment. Words, when understood, indicate a structure. Whatever is understood implies a meaning. Now, whether or not is it the intended meaning is another question. Meaning evolves from the sentence as it is. What it says may not be what it means. Understanding evolves from the mind in reaction to what is being said. The distinction is not between the sentence and what it means, but what it intends. We raise this question, does the sentence say what it means thereby describing its intention? It is the mind which makes this distinction. The mind recognizes that to truly understand, it must understand intention. Only in this way does a sentence belong to logic.

A sentence belongs to logic when the facts which make it true or false are understood because the mind has experienced their experiential value. This is the test to determine whether a sentence is really cognitive. Facts are based on intention; for the mind to actualize the relationships which make it possible to realize the dependency factors upon which every fact is based, is to structure "criteria for cognitivity." What makes a sentence true or false is the fact. The sentence, to be logical, must intend the fact. This is what the mind must understand in order to find meaning. For the mind to believe the sentence is not enough. It must know why it believes it; it is not the sentence which expresses belief; rather, it is the mind which reacts in belief or disbelief. The fact must become the essence of belief. It is the analysis of the fact in sentence which determines the truth of the proposition. The intentional inference of fact is the problem which the mind must solve as it is confronted by the sentence. It is a matter of deriving meaning from experiencing the potentiality of the intentional inference of the fact. Meaning evolves from the concepts derived from the ideas contained in words in relation to one another.

Rather than falling prey to Russell's logic, we suggest the following: a sentence is meaningful when the mind has experienced the intent of its words functioning as facts, and validated the dependency relationships between the words as they express the logicality of the "syntactical relations to one or more epistemologically basic proposition."

SELECT BIBLIOGRAPHY

Ackermann, Robert. *Theories of Knowledge.* New York: McGraw-Hill Book Company, 1965.

Aquinas, Thomas. *The Summa Theologica.* 3 Vols. New York: Benziger Brothers, Inc., 1947.

Aristotle. *Organon and On The Soul* In *The Basic Works of Aristotle.* Edited by Richard McKeon. New York: Random House, 1941.

Augustine. *Confessions.* New York: Fathers of the Church, Inc., 1953.

Ayer, A. J. *Language, Truth and Logic.* New York: Dover Publications, Inc., 1952.

———. *The Problem of Knowledge.* Baltimore: Penguin Books, 1956.

Bacon, Francis. *Advancement of Learning and Novum Organum.* Edited by J. Creighton. New York: Colonial Publishing Inc., 1900.

Bergson, H. *An Introduction to Metaphysics.* Translated by T. E. Hulme. New York: G. P. Putnam's Sons, 1912.

———. *Creative Mind.* Translated by M. L. Andison. New York: Philosophical Library, Inc., 1946.

Berkeley, George. *A Treatise Concerning the Principles of Human Knowledge.* Indianapolis: Bobbs-Merrill Co., Inc., 1957.

Blackstone, William T. *The Problem of Religious Knowledge.* New Jersey: Prentice-Hall, Inc. (A Spectrum Book), 1963.

Boas, George. *The Limits of Reason.* London: Routledge and Kegan Paul, 1961.

Bom, Max. *The Restless Universe.* 2nd rev. ed. New York: Dover Publications Inc., 1957.

Broad, C. L. *Scientific Thought.* New Jersey: Littlefield, Adams and Co., 1959.

Select Bibliography

Bronowski, J. *Science and Human Values.* New York: Harper and Row (A Harper Torch Book), 1959.

Bruno, Giordano. *Cause, Principle and Unity.* Translated by J. Lindsay. New York: International Publishers, 1962.

Burtt, E. A. *The Metaphysical Foundations of Modem Science.* Garden City: Doubleday and Company, Inc. (Anchor Books), 1932.

Capaldi, Nicholas. *Human Knowledge.* New York: Pegasus, 1969.

Carnap, Rudolph. *Introduction to Symbolic Logic and Its Applications.* New York: Dover Publications, Inc., 1958.

Cassirer, Ernest. *The Problem of Knowledge.* New Haven: Yale University Press, 1950.

———. *An Essay On Man.* Garden City: Doubleday and Company, Inc. (Doubleday Anchor Books), 1956.

Chapman, Harmon M. *Sensations and Phenomenology.* Bloomington: Indiana University Press, 1966.

Childe, V. G. *Society and Knowledge.* New York: Harper and Brothers, 1956.

Comford, Francis M. *Plato's Theory of Knowledge.* London: Routledge and Kegan Paul, 1967.

Descartes, Rene. *The Philosophical Works.* 2 Vols. Cambridge: Cambridge University Press, 1968.

Dewey, John. *How We Think.* Boston: D. C. Heath and Company, 1933.

———. *Experience and Nature.* New York: Dover Publications, Inc., 1958.

———. *The Quest for Certainty.* New York: G. P. Putnam's Sons (Capricorn Books), 1960.

Dewey, John and Bentley, Arthur F. *Knowing and the Known.* Boston:

Select Bibliography

Beacon Press, 1949.

Ducasse, Curt J. *Causation and The Types of Necessity.* New York: Dover Publications Inc., 1969.

du Noüy, Pierre Lecomte. *The Road to Reason.* New York: Longmans, Green and Company, 1949.

———. *Between Knowing and Believing.* New York: David McKay, Inc., 1966.

Eddington, A. *The Nature of the Physical World.* New York: Macmillan Company, 1929.

———. *Philosophy of Physical Science.* Ann Arbor: University of Michigan Press, 1958.

Einstein, A. *Essays in Science.* Translated by Alan Harris. New York: Philosophical Library, Inc., 1953.

Farber, Marvin. *Basic Issues of Philosophy.* New York: Harper and Row (A Harper Torchbook), 1968.

Fichte, Johann Gottlieb. *Science of Knowledge.* New York: Appleton Century-Crofts, 1970.

Gallagher, Kenneth T. *The Philosophy of Knowledge.* New York: Sheed and Ward, 1964.

Guzie, Tad W. *The Analogy of Learning.* New York: Sheed and Ward, 1960.

Hammond, Albert L. *Ideas About Substance.* Baltimore: John Hopkins Press, 1969.

Hartnack, Justus. *Theory of Knowledge.* New York: Harcourt, Brace and World, Inc. (An Original Harbinger Book), 1967.

Hawkins, D. J. B. *Being and Becoming.* London: Sheed and Ward, 1954.

Heidegger, Martin. *An Introduction to Metaphysics.* Garden City:

Select Bibliography

Doubleday and Company (Anchor Books), 1961.

———. *Kant and the Problem of Metaphysics.* Bloomington: Indiana University Press, 1962.

———. *Discourse on Thinking.* New York: Harper and Row (A Harper Torchbook), 1969.

Hintikica, Jaakko. *Knowledge and Belief.* Ithaca: Cornell University Press, 1962.

Hobhouse, L. T. *The Theory of Knowledge.* London: Methuen, 1921.

Hook, Sidney. *The Quest For Being.* New York: Dell Publishing Company (A Delta Book), 1963.

Hume, David. *An Inquiry Concerning Human Understanding.* Indianapolis: Bobbs-Merrill, Inc., 1955.

Husserl, Edmund. *Ideas: General Introduction to Pure Phenomenology.* Translated by W. R. Boyce Gibson. New York: Macmillan Company, 1952.

James, William. *Pragmatism.* New York: Meridan Books, 1955.

Joad, C. E. M. *Philosophical Aspects of Modem Science.* New York: Barnes and Noble, Inc., 1964.

Jones, Philip Chapin. *The Nature of Knowledge.* New York: Scarecrow Press, Inc., 1964.

Kant, Immanuel. *Critique of Pure Reason.* 2nd Ed. Translated by F. Max Muller. New York: Macmillan Company, 1934.

Kierkegaard, S. *Concluding Unscientific Postscript.* Translated by D. F. Swenson. Princeton: Princeton University Press, 1944.

Köhler, Wolfgang. *The Place of Value in A World of Facts.* New York: New American Library (A Mentor Book), 1966.

Lazowiek, Frank E. *The Science of Philosophy.* New York: Philosophical Library, 1959.

Select Bibliography

Leibniz, G. W. *Discourse on Metaphysics in Philosophical Writings of G. Leibniz.* Translated by Mary Morris. New York: E. P. Dutton and Company, Inc. (Everyman's Library), 1934.

Lewis, Clarence Irving. *Mind and the World-Order.* New York: Scribner's, 1929.

Locke, John. *An Essay Concerning Human Understanding.* 2 Vols. New York: Dover Publications, Inc., 1959.

Lynch, William F. *The Integrating Mind.* New York: Sheed and Ward, 1962.

Macintosh, Douglas C. *The Problem of Knowledge.* New York: Macmillan Company, 1915.

Maisels, M. *Thought and Truth.* London: Vision Press Limited, n.d.

Malcolm, Norman. *Knowledge and Certainty.* New Jersey: Prentice-Hall, Inc., 1963.

———. *Problems of Mind.* New York: Harper and Row (A Harper Torchbook), 1971.

Mannheim, Karl. *Ideology and Utopia.* New York: Harcourt, Brace and Company (A Harvest Book), 1936.

Maritain, J. *The Philosophy of Nature.* New York: Philosophical Library, Inc., 1951.

———. *The Degrees of Knowledge.* Translated by G. B. Phelan. New York: Scribner's, 1959.

Martin, W. O. *The Order and Integration of Knowledge.* Ann Arbor: University of Michigan Press, 1957.

Mill, John Stuart. *A System of Logic.* 8th Ed. New York: Longmans, Green and Company, Inc., 1929.

Moore, G. E. *Philosophical Studies.* New Jersey: Littlefield, Adams and Co., 1968

Select Bibliography

Newman, John Henry. *Grammar of Assent.* New York: Doubleday and Company (Image), 1955.

Paul, Leslie. *The Meaning of Human Existence.* London: Faber and Faber, 1949.

Pears, David. *What is Knowledge?* New York: Harper and Row (A Harper Torchbook), 1971.

Plato. *Timaeus, Gorgios, and Theaetetus.* In *The Dialogues of Plato.* Edited by Benjamin Jowett. 2 Vols. New York: Random House, 1937.

Poincare, Henri. *Science and Hypothesis.* New York: Dover Publications, Inc., 1952.

———. *Science and Method.* New York: Dover Publications, Inc., 1958.

Polanyi, Michael. *Personal Knowledge.* New York: Harper and Row (A Harper Torchbook), 1964.

———. *Science, Faith and Society.* Chicago: University of Chicago Press (Phoenix Books), 1964.

Popper, Karl. *The Poverty of Historicism.* New York: Harper and Row (A Harper Torchbook), 1964.

———. *The Logic of Scientific Discovery.* New York: Harper and Row (A Harper Torchbook), 1965.

———. *Conjectures and Refutations.* New York: Harper and Row (A Harper Torchbook), 1968.

Regis, L. M. *St. Thomas and Epistemology.* Milwaukee: Marquette University Press, 1946.

———. *Epistemology.* New York: Macmillian Company, 1964.

Royce, Josiah. *Principles of Logic.* New York: Philosophical Library (Wisdom Library), 1961.

Select Bibliography

Russell, Bertrand. *An Inquiry into Meaning and Truth.* Baltimore: Penguin Books, 1962.

———. *Mysticism and Logic.* New York: Barnes and Noble, Inc., 1963.

———. *Human Knowledge.* New York; Simon and Schuster, 1964.

———. *Logic and Knowledge.* R. E. Marsh. London: Macmillian Company, 1964.

Ryle, Gilbert. *The Concept of Mind.* New York: Barnes and Noble, Inc., 1949.

Santayana, George. *Scepticism and Animal Faith.* New York: Dover Publications, Inc., 1955.

Sayre, Kenneth M. *Consciousness.* New York: Random House, 1969.

Scheffler, Israel. *Conditions of Knowledge.* Chicago: Scott, Foresman and Co., 1965.

Schon, Donald A. *Invention and the Evolution of Ideas.* London: Social Science Paperbooks, 1963.

Spinoza, B. B. *On the Improvement of the Understanding.* In *The Chief Works of Benedict de Spinoza.* Translated by R. H. M. Elives. 2 Vols. New York: Dover Publications, Inc., 1951.

Steenberghen, Fernand van. *Epistemology.* New York: Joseph F. Wagner, Inc., 1949.

Stevenson, Charles L. *Facts and Values.* New Haven: Yale University Press, 1963.

Swartz, Robert J., ed. *Perceiving, Sensing and Knowing.* New York: Doubleday and Company, Inc. (Anchor Books), 1965.

Tomlin, E. W. F. *Living and Knowing.* London: Faber and Faber, 1955.

Toulmin, Stephen. *Foresight and Understanding.* New York: Harper and Row (A Harper Torchbook), 1963.

Select Bibliography

Von Wright, Georg Henrik. *A Treatise on Induction and Probability.* New Jersey: Littlefield, Adams and Co., 1960.

Watkin, E. I. *A Philosophy of Form.* London: Sheed and Ward, 1950.

Weigel, Gustav, S. J. and Madden, Arthur G. *Knowledge, Its Values and Limits.* New Jersey: Prentice-Hall, Inc. (A Spectrum Book), 1961.

Werkmeister, W. H. *The Basis and Structure of Knowledge.* New York: Harper and Brothers, 1948.

Whitehead, A. N. *The Concept of Nature.* Ann Arbor: University of Michigan Press, 1957.

―――. *Process and Reality.* New York: Harper and Row (A Harper Torchbook), 1960.

―――. *Modes of Thought.* New York: Free Press, 1968.

Windelband, Wilhelm. *Theories in Logic.* New York: Citadel Press, 1961.

Wisdom, John. *Problems of Mind and Matter.* Cambridge: Cambridge University Press, 1963.

Wittgenstein, L. *The Blue and Brown Books.* Oxford: Blackwell, 1958.

―――. *Philosophical Investigations.* Translated by G. E. M. Anscombe. 2nd ed. Oxford: Blackwell, 1958.

Woozley, A. D. *Theory of Knowledge.* New York: Barnes and Noble, Inc., 1966.

Yolton, John W. *Theory of Knowledge.* New York: Macmillan Company, 1965.

Znaniecki, Florian. *The Social Role of the Man of Knowledge.* New York: Harper and Row (A Harper Torchbook), 1968.

Resources

Favor

If you enjoyed this book, may I ask a small favor? Please go back to Amazon and leave an honest review of *An Introduction to Theory of Knowledge*. Reviews help us spread the word of Russell A. Peterson to the world more effectively, and sustain our efforts. We appreciate your continued support.

Thank you,
Barry J. Peterson

Additional Reading Resources:

The Power of I AM
A compilation of the best *I AM* quotes
www.ThePowerofIAM.org
Compiled & Edited by David Allen

Reading to the Dead: A Transitional Grief Therapy for the Living
www.ReadingToTheDead.com
Author: Barry J. Peterson

Neville Goddard: The Complete Reader
Includes all 10 of Neville's spiritual classics in one book
www.NevilleGoddardReader.com

www.NevilleGoddardFreeLectures.com
Over 125 Free Audio Lectures in Neville Goddard's Voice
www.TheNevilleGoddardProject.org

www.AudioEnlightenment.com (Membership Website)
The largest repository of Neville Goddard resources on the internet
www.AudioEnlightenmentPress.com

www.ingramcontent.com/pod-product-compliance
Lightning Source LLC
Chambersburg PA
CBHW032024230426
43671CB00005B/191